BLACKBELT IN BLACKJACK

PLAYING 21 AS A MARTIAL ART

By Arnold Snyder

♣♦♠♥

414 Santa Clara Avenue
Oakland, CA 94610

Front Cover: Ed Cassel
Book Design & Layout: Robt. A. Hover

Copyright © 1983 by Arnold Snyder

Portions of this book have previously appeared in different form in the following periodicals: *Gambling Times, Boardwalker International, Rouge et Noir News,* and *The Experts Blackjack Newsletter.* Copyright © 1980, 1981, 1982 by Arnold Snyder

Snyder, Arnold.
   Blackbelt in Blackjack: Playing 21 As A Martial Art.
First Printing: April, 1983
Second Printing: October, 1983

Library of Congress Catalog Card Number: 82-83160

ISBN 0-910575-02-9

Printed in the United States of America

CONTENTS

ACKNOWLEDGEMENTS

I would like to thank:

Crazy Bob
Julian Braun
Clarke Cant
Sam Case
Paul Dayton
Doug Finlay
Bob Fisher
Axel Freed
Bill Gaem
Brian Gothberg
Peter Griffin
John Gwynn
Brooklyn Mike
Jerry Patterson
Stanley Roberts
J.S.
Don Schlesinger
Bonnie St. Eiger
Ralph Stricker
Stanford Wong

For valuable contributions.   —A.S.

DEDICATION

This book is dedicated to two phenomenal women, neither of whom are blackjack players. First and foremost I would like to dedicate this book to Alison Finlay, my indefatigable editor, morale booster, decision maker, problem solver, spirit lifter and crisis eliminator. Without Alison's time, care, and patience, my unfortunate readers would be sloughing through my indecipherable grammar, my circumlocutious verbosity, my exasperating redundancies, and my bombastic pseudo-erudition. Because of Alison's merciful blue pencil, the reader has been spared sentences like the previous one throughout the remainder of this text.

This book is also dedicated to Carol Portice Harris, who at one time instructed me in the art of karate. When I began my instruction, I was 28 years old, 6 feet tall, and weighed about 170 lbs. Carol was about 35, 5'4" and weighed about 115 lbs. On my first day of instruction, she asked me to spar with her. I was told to throw punches and kicks, and to attempt to block her attacks. Looking at her, a small, softspoken woman, I thought to myself, "I'd better go easy on her. If I land a punch, it would kill her!" Within 60 seconds, without ever touching me, Carol radically altered my consciousness. I knew beyond any shadow of a doubt that my life was at this woman's mercy. Carol taught me that appearances can be deceiving, and that the big guy doesn't always win. ♣♦♠♥

1

There are only two games offered in American casinos which can be consistently beaten legally. One is poker. The other is blackjack. Blackjack systems are based primarily on mathematics, though psychology plays an increasingly important part.

Little is known of the original blackjack systems. In *Beat The Dealer* (1962, Random House), Dr. Edward O. Thorp discusses a number of the first systems developers, who had colorful names like "Greasy John" and "System Smitty". They had privately worked out crude but effective blackjack strategies with which they'd won a livelihood from the Las Vegas blackjack tables. Until the early sixties, and the publication of Dr. Thorp's book, the casinos were unaware that blackjack could be beaten by any system, so players who were applying systematic winning methods were viewed as lucky suckers, who would, in the long run, lose their shirts like all the other gamblers and system players who frequented the casinos.

In 1956, a group of mathematicians first applied the methods of statistical analysis to the game of blackjack, and developed a "basic strategy" which they published in a technical journal for mathematicians. This strategy, if followed rigorously, would narrow the house edge, making black-jack close to a break even proposition for the player, over the long run. Though a colloquial version of this paper was later published, few gamblers took notice. Gamblers wanted *winning* systems, not "break even" systems.

One person who took particular note of this technical paper was Dr. Edward O. Thorp, a mathematician. He saw that this strategy had been tediously computed on old-fashioned calculators. He had access to what, in the early sixties, was a sophisticated computer. He wrote a more precise program than had been used for the original basic strategy, and subsequently developed a more accurate strategy. Blackjack is a difficult game to analyze mathematically, because the depletion of the deck, as cards are played, constantly alters the makeup of the remaining deck, thus constantly altering the probabilities of making a hand or busting, winning or losing. It occurred to Dr. Thorp that, using a computer, he could analyze just how the makeup of the deck affected the possible outcomes of the various hands. His method was unique. He wrote a program to analyze the player's best strategy and long run expectation, assuming various cards in turn had been removed from the deck. He noted that the player's chance of winning was dramatically increased when fives were removed from the deck. In fact, to remove any of the "low" cards—2, 3, 4, 5, 6 or 7—was advantageous to the player in varying degrees. On the other hand, if tens or aces were removed, the player's chances were hurt quite dramatically.

Thorp's first winning strategy was based on counting fives. He recommended betting heavily when they were depleted, and also playing a slightly different strategy when no fives were in the deck. His next system—and this is

INTRODUCTION

3

the system upon which most winning card-counting systems in use today are based—was called the "ten-count". In this system, tens and non-tens were counted separately. Larger bets were placed as the proportion of tens to non-tens in the deck became larger.

The ten-count system, as Thorp created it, was not easy to learn nor to apply in a casino. It required keeping two separate "backward" counts, and computing a ratio prior to betting and strategy decisions. Thorp played his system with what today would be considered a wild betting strategy, sometimes jumping from a table-minimum bet of a dollar, to a table-maximum of $500. Casinos were unaware of the power of Thorp's system, and many continued dealing their single-deck hand-held games down to the last card. Players capable of using Thorp's system accurately had an enormous advantage over the house. Players who were capable of following even a crude approximation of Thorp's strategy could win big if they used a large enough betting spread.

Once the Las Vegas casinos realized a legitimate winning system was being employed at their blackjack tables, they took drastic action. They changed the rules of the game. This was in 1964, eight years after the first publication of a relatively accurate basic strategy, and two years after the original publication of Thorp's *Beat The Dealer*.

The rule changes did not last long because, to the casinos' dismay, players stayed away from the tables in droves, rather than play against the new rules. Casinos began losing a lot of money. So, bracing themselves for the worst, they changed back to the original rules.

The worst never came. In fact, the opposite occurred. Blackjack became the most popular table game in U.S. casinos. Everyone, it seemed, believed they could beat the game, but few put in the time and effort to learn a legitimate system. Many blackjack systems were sold which were not mathematically valid. Many players who did have valid systems had no understanding of normal fluctuation. They "overbet" their limited bankrolls and "tapped out" before they ever had a chance to see the "long run" profits. Most importantly, casinos learned to recognize card counters by their style.

Card counters "jumped" their bets suddenly. They paid inordinate amounts of attention to everybody's cards. They were quiet. They concentrated. They didn't drink or socialize. They were often young collegiate types who didn't fit in with the normal run of tourists and vacationing businessmen.

Once spotted, a suspected card counter would be silently observed by the pit boss or "eye in the sky." If suspicions were confirmed, the dealer would be signaled to "shuffle-up" on the counter. If the suspect changed tables, the "heat" would follow him. If he did not leave the casino, he would be asked to leave, and ultimately ordered to leave.

Thus, the casinos weeded out the few competent players, and let the hoards of fools who thought they could beat the tables with sloppy play and invalid systems play to their heart's content.

A small number of card counters have been able to continue to profit from the game of blackjack. Two factors contribute to the success of the present day counter. First of all, he knows the basic math of the game. He has studied the game and various valid systems and has a realistic attitude about his long and short run expectations. Secondly, he knows the basic psychology of the casino environment. He understands how casinos detect counters, and so disguises his play. He is an actor. If he senses heat, he leaves, perhaps to return at a different time, when different casino personnel are running the show. He doesn't take chances. There are lots of casinos.

Although two decades have passed since the first valid card counting system was published, many casinos still offer beatable blackjack games. The "math" aspect of card counting is easier than ever. The systems presented in this book are among the easiest-to-learn professional level systems ever devised. This does not mean that you can learn to beat the game of blackjack in an hour. If you are serious about playing blackjack for profit, you should plan to spend quite a bit of time at study and practice to develop your proficiency. I will say this, however: *any person with average math ability could learn to count cards at a professional level.*

The difficulty of making money as a card counter is not math, but psychology. Some people are good actors. Some are not. Some are very perceptive of others' attitudes and are capable of manipulating people. Some cannot do this. To make it as a card counter, you must often be sociable and friendly to dealers and pit bosses while simultaneously deceiving them into thinking you're just another dumb gambler. Most card counters who experience any long term success thrive on this exhilarating espionage-like aspect of the game. You must be part rogue and part charlatan. You must be cool under pressure. You must have enough money behind you to weather losing streaks without financial worry. You must be confident, smart, fast, perceptive, even brave. You must thrill to beating the casinos at their own game. If you're not in it for the fun, as much as for the money, you'll never make it as a counter. Card counting is boring, once mastered. It's a lot of work. Few who try card counting stick with it. It's like most games—chess, tennis, even the stock market; many people "know how to play", but only a few become masters.

This book is titled *"Blackbelt in Blackjack: Playing 21 as a Martial Art."* Many of the same talents, skills and virtues which would earn you a top ranking position in any of the martial arts could also be applied to casino blackjack. The concept of card counting is based on *balance*, and making your attack when you are in the stronger position. You never make yourself vulnerable to your opponent (the casino), but through your superior knowledge of your opponent's weaknesses (rules, conditions, cards remaining to be played, etc.), you allow your opponent to bring about his own loss. Your strategy is based on *simplicity*, not complexity. You take no foolish chances. What moves you make are made with precision, with force ($), and perfect timing. Your opponent thinks he can beat you, thinks he *is* beating you, and does not see the strength of your superior position. You make your moves with a natural ease. Your camouflage, which allows you to win, is your ability to appear as if you are not even trying.

I realize that most of the readers of this book will not go on to become masters of blackjack strategy. With this in mind, I will offer many simplified, albeit less powerful, methods that the casual player may use to better his chances of winning at the blackjack tables. I will also attempt to provide clear explanations of the more powerful techniques, so that the casual player will at least understand how and why the advanced systems work. By understanding these concepts, a beginning player who has not developed the skill to apply them will, hopefully, realize his limited abilities, and will not entertain false visions of himself as an unbeatable player.

One thing you must remember: *Casinos don't give money away.* You have to take it. And contrary to appearances, casinos are holding on to their money with both fists. You've got to be slick to take on the casinos for high stakes, and walk away with your shirt.

♣♦♠♥

BLACKBELT IN BLACKJACK

PLAYING 21 AS A MARTIAL ART

Bishop Synder inaugurates the first church of blackjack on October 25, 1981, at Caesars Tahoe Casino, Stateline, Nevada.

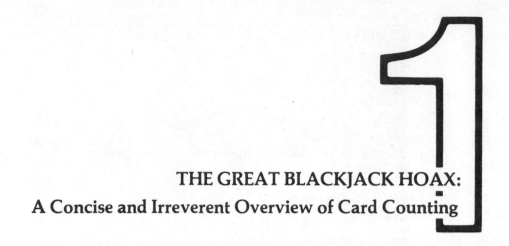

THE GREAT BLACKJACK HOAX:
A Concise and Irreverent Overview of Card Counting

The First Church of Blackjack

> *"My People! I have a vision! I see the dawning of the Age of Blackjack! I see a world with a casino on every street! From Atlantic City to L.A.! New York! Chicago! Your Town! My Town! I see a world where dealers make housecalls! Welcome, my people to Blackjack Heaven!"*

So began my address inaugurating the First Church of Blackjack. It was Sunday morning, October 25, 1981. The half-hour ceremony which introduced the Twenty-One Commandments and ended with the Blessing of the Chips took place in the main conference hall of Caesars Tahoe Casino in Stateline, Nevada.

> *"I see a world where pit bosses direct traffic on the green felt streets! Where towering stacks of multi-colored chips line the pavement like so many lawn ornaments! Lucky Bucks in every pocket! A cocktail waitress in every garage!"*

The First Church of Blackjack is one of the fastest growing religions in the world today. We increased our flock 500 fold in the first six months alone. As the only Bishop in the church hierarchy, this pleases me.

9

"Onward Blackjack Soldiers,
Counting down the deck!
Never be a loser;
You can win your bet!
You can beat the dealer,
Leave him in disgrace!
You can make the pit boss wish
He'd never seen your face!

You'll go out with the cocktail waitress
When she sees your bread!
Even though the management
Would rather see you dead!
Just send me your money and
I'll show you how to win!
Cash or check or MasterCard,
You'll never lose again!

Onward Blackjack Soldiers!
You can't get nothin' for free;
If you donate to my church,
You'll soon get rich like me!"

The First Church of Blackjack is, of course, a joke. My performance as "Bishop Snyder" was sponsored by the University of Nevada. The event was listed as a "parody" in the official outline of symposiums which were presented at the Fifth National Conference on Gambling and Risk-Taking. Yet, joke or not, the church's membership is growing by leaps and bounds. There's money in blackjack.

Twenty years ago, the number one casino table game in this country, in terms of gross revenues for the casinos, was craps. This was not surprising. Craps was an All American pastime during World War II. The State of Nevada provided a way for old war buddies to get together and shoot dice through the years. Look at any craps table today and you'll find an inordinate proportion of rowdy men in their late fifties and early sixties, hooting and howling like a bunch of 19-year-old G.I.'s on leave.

Today, thanks to Ed Thorp, casinos make their money from blackjack players. They make a lot of money from card counters. Authors and systems sellers make a lot of money from blackjack players who are, or want to be, card counters. Card counting is big business, but the people who make the most money from it are not the card counters. The greatest profit from card counting goes to the casinos. Systems sellers come in a distant second as far as blackjack profits go. Card counters, as a group, are suffering a steadily increasing loss from their blackjack investments of time and money.

"I was once like you, my friend! I was tired! I was hungry! I was cold! I had no shoes on my feet! Then I found BLACKJACK! You must ask yourselves, my people, are you prepared to take God's gamble? Look deep inside your hearts, brothers and sisters! Are you ready for the Holy Risk?"

A Card Counter Is Born

I am a card counter. I got hooked on blackjack four years ago to the point of obsession. I love this game. There is nothing as exciting as beating a casino and walking out the door with more money in your pockets than when you entered. Card counting offers a legitimate thrill. To enter a casino with the ability to beat the house, knowing the casino will be doing everything it can to identify and eliminate such a threat, gives a James-Bond-Spy-vs.-Spy flavor to the experience. The heart races. The feeling is not unlike that which I recall from my childhood when all the kids in my neighborhood would choose up sides for "cops and robbers". I'd forgotten how much fun it was to hide, sneak, run, hold your breath in anticipation... Adults don't play that way, except for maybe a few real cops and robbers.

Then I discovered card counting. It took me a year of weekend trips to Nevada, some dozen books on card counting, and another half-dozen books on mathematics, to learn that I didn't have enough money to play the game professionally. Many blackjack authors seemed to neglect the risk factor. The counter's edge is extremely small. The fluctuation of capital is very great. If you do not have a lot of money, you will not last.

I'll never forget my first trip to Nevada as a card counter. I was driving a car that was 15 years old and over-the-hill. It not only guzzled gas but leaked oil. Winding up through the Sierra Nevada mountains on my way to Lake Tahoe and the casinos of Stateline, I had to stop twice to add a quart of oil, and give to my overheated wreck a rest. I was with a friend, and we were splitting the cost of the trip. The way we figured it, after paying for gas, oil, motel room and meals, we'd have about $55 left over to play at the blackjack tables. When I pulled over to the shoulder of the road for my second oil stop, I said to my friend, "It's hard to believe that we're on our way to becoming wealthy. I hope my car makes it up this damn mountain."

"A year from now," my friend responded, "you'll look back on this day and laugh. This is just the beginning."

One year and some dozen trips to Nevada later, I thought back to that first trip and I laughed. I was again on my way to Stateline, this time alone. My car had long since broken down, beyond repair, and I didn't have the money for another car. I was traveling by bus, and the way I figured it, if I was ahead by twenty-five bucks the first day, I could get a motel room and stay for another day. Otherwise, it was back to the Greyhound station that night. About that time I started to realize I'd been deluding myself into believing I'd get rich at this card game.

Why Blackjack Is so Popular

Blackjack has become the casinos' number one money making table game precisely because people believe the game can be beaten. Casinos are forever bemoaning their losses to card counters. They are constantly changing their rules to make their games tougher for these feared blackjack "experts". Casino floormen, with increasing frequency, ceremoniously bar suspected counters from their tables. Projecting this image of "counter paranoia" is one of the most successful advertising campaigns ever developed. Not one person in a thousand has what it takes to make any significant amount of money playing blackjack, but hundreds of thousands of people have given it a try. Card counting is not difficult for the dedicated practitioner, but few people are dedicated enough, and, as most players discover the hard way, there is more to being a successful card counter than the ability to count cards.

In cynical moments, I see the American public being taken for a ride by the curiously combined forces of the casino industry and the blackjack systems sellers. A tremendous effort is being made to convince people that card counters can get rich quick at the casino blackjack tables.

Many of the biggest and most prestigious publishing houses list books on card counting in their catalogues. Card counting programs are available for most home computers and in most home video formats. Blackjack "schools" and seminars are churning out thousands of graduates per month. Tuitions often run as high as $1,000.

I don't mean to imply that all blackjack systems sellers are trying to bilk the public. I am a systems seller. I'm the author of three books on casino blackjack, numerous technical papers, and a quarterly journal for professional and aspiring professional counters. I've written operating manuals for two home computer blackjack programs, and articles on card counting for numerous periodicals. I've acted as informal consultant for a number of high stakes international counting teams. I *know* the game can be beaten. I know many part-time card counters who regularly beat the tables for significant amounts of money. I know a few players who have made a fortune playing blackjack. But these successful pros are few and far between. Their dedication to the game is beyond that of the average counter. They live and breathe blackjack. They devour every written word on the subject. They drill and practice until they are counting cards in their sleep. They view professional blackjack as a dog-eat-dog business, which it is.

Many blackjack system authors are honest about their negative experiences at the black-jack tables. Most publishers, however, do not advertise this aspect of the game, nor does the media in general pay it much heed. It's not newsworthy to say, "Gambler loses money." Advertisements for blackjack systems promise everything from instant wealth to private airplanes and islands! I know of one well-known author who has publicly castigated his publisher for what he felt were "questionable" promotional tactics. After reading the ad, I agreed that the publisher's integrity was sadly lacking. Later, after speaking with the publisher, I realized that he viewed himself as a sincere and honest businessman, trying to promote a product he believed in, to the best of his ability. He explained how he'd hired the best copy-writer in the business to write the ads for the book. He'd put much personal time and effort into making this book the biggest, best, and most comprehensive text on professional card counting ever published. He succeeded. The book became a best seller. But now the author was complaining about the promotional tactics that had made his book a success.

Copywriters promote everything from toothpaste to automobiles by selling a lifestyle that supposedly goes along with the product. Blackjack systems promoters use the same methods. For many people, buying a book on how to count cards may not be any different from buying toothpaste. They've lived too long to believe in advertising claims.

To be disappointed with your toothpaste, however, is no big thing. To be disillusioned with your blackjack system can be devastating. I've received letters from card counters complaining of heavy losses at the blackjack tables. They want to know what they're doing wrong. In many cases, these players are simply placing bets that are too high for their limited bankrolls. Some players have had their savings wiped out in a period of weeks or months.

Many authors are less than candid about their personal experiences. Some books on card counting are deceptive, claiming that anyone with two weeks practice can be a blackjack pro, never even mentioning the possibility of loss. The major publishers of blackjack books are unfamiliar with card counting, casino conditions, and blackjack systems. Numerous popular books on card counting contain gross misinformation in the form of "blurbs" on their covers—over which the authors have no control. I know of one highly respected author who discovered errors in his published work, but through many years of reprints his publisher has refused to correct the text because of the typesetting expense. I know of one authority who supplied his publisher with all the technical data for his counting system, with the under-standing that his publisher would ghost-write the basic text and anecdotal material to fill out the book. To this author's chagrin, the publisher took it upon himself to write one of the most important chapters in this book, the chapter on betting strategy, effectively altering the author's winning system to a worthless exercise in gambling.

The average player has no way of knowing that the author of his system disagrees with the publisher's advertising claims, or large portions of the text. The most respected names in the field of blackjack literature have been abused by their publishers, promoters and imitators.

Compound all of this misinformation about card counting with the dozens of books on the market which teach totally inaccurate strategies, "money management" systems, systems so weak as to be a complete waste of time, or too difficult for human players to master, and you can begin to fathom why card counting is the best thing that every happened to the casino industry in this country.

"Dear Bishop Snyder,

"I have been faithfully following your Holy Road to Riches Program, but try as I might to Beat the Dealer, I cannot. I have already lost my life savings, my house, my car, and, God forbid, my credit line at Harvey's. I am beginning to think that the only way to Beat the Dealer is to wait for him out in the parking lot with a tire iron. Please, Your Most Holiness, help me before I do something drastic. Do you have a system for roulette?

"Losing My Faith and Everything Else in Las Vegas"

Today, blackjack profits account for more than 25% of the casinos' gross revenues from gaming. Since 1963, the percentage increase in the number of blackjack games available in Nevada's casinos has been more than three times greater than the percentage increase in all other games combined. In 1981, American casinos reported a gross win at their blackjack tables alone of almost one billion dollars ($938,884,880, according to the combined published data of the New Jersey Casino Control Commission and the Nevada Gaming Control Board).

The Future of Blackjack

In Atlantic City, blackjack pro Ken Uston won his case against the casinos. The casinos may no longer bar skillful players from their tables, so a new experiment is beginning. Some casinos are going to attempt to employ rules and procedures which will make the game of blackjack virtually unbeatable for all card counters. Many Nevada casinos currently offer blackjack games which are unprofitable for card counters. Most card counters are unaware of this. Many popular books on card counting make scant mention of the importance of "table conditions" to profit potential. In a move to go beyond the worst games offered in Nevada, the New Jersey Casino Control Commission has given the Atlantic City casinos permission to use "double" shoes, with as many as eight decks shuffled together in a single shoe, and to use an experimental "continuous" shuffling procedure throughout the game. These conditions would make the game of blackjack a losing proposition for even a computer, let alone any human system player. True to form, however, the Atlantic City casino executives are already moaning that these changes will not protect them from skillful players. The casinos, naturally, want players to believe that this unbeatable sucker trap is still a game of skill. It is common knowledge among casino executives that hopeful card counters and other blackjack system players are their main source of income, assuming most casino executives read their own financial statements. If card counters actually stopped playing blackjack in Atlantic City, the casinos would die. The casinos may well get away with this ruse, at least for awhile. The American public *believes* blackjack can be beaten, unaware of the effects of new procedures. Many unscrupulous systems sellers will undoubtedly continue to hype their wares, as always, without mentioning the games which are not beatable. The casinos will continue to moan about their losses to counters, as if every other person at their tables were getting rich. But you can't fool all of the people all of the time. If the skill factor is permanently removed, the game will die, and the casinos will suffer the most. I do not believe the casino industry will let this happen.

The Great Blackjack Myth

What many people (including card counters, system sellers, dealers, pit bosses, and the media at large) fail to comprehend, is that to be a successful professional card counter takes no less ability, study, dedication, time and luck than any other profession, be it law, real estate, or architectural engineering. Few people have what it takes to master any of these professions. Card counting is simply attempting to inconspicuously, legally, and consistently, siphon large sums of money from a multi-billion dollar industry that is using the most advanced surveillance techniques this side of the Pentagon.

Most card counters believe in the Great Blackjack Myth that flatly states: *A card counter can beat the game of casino blackjack*. The truth is that *some* card counting strategies can beat *some* blackjack games, depending on the number of decks being shuffled together, the number of players at the table, the number of cards being dealt out prior to reshuffling, the rule variations, the betting spread being employed, the size of the counter's bankroll, etc. The threat of being barred causes many counters to kill their own chances of winning. Counters seek out more crowded, less conspicuous tables. They hold down their betting spreads. They make occasional "dumb" playing decisions. All of these camouflage tactics cut into, and often kill, the counter's potential small edge.

Card counters, as a subculture, have developed a unique jargon. One term that all counters understand is "heat". *Heat* is a pit boss breathing down your neck, a dealer shuffling the cards any time you raise your bet, or, worst of all, a floorman "reading your rights", i.e., "You may play any of the casino games *except* blackjack; if you attempt to place a bet at any blackjack table, you may be arrested for trespassing."

Many counters think they're getting away with murder when they don't get heat from casinos. The truth is that the casinos are swarming with counters, and most counters are easily detectable. By standing behind crowded blackjack tables, and counting down the cards as they are dealt, I can spot many obvious card counters in the course of a few hours. If I can spot them so easily, you can be sure the casinos can spot them. Most counters follow betting schemes that stick out glaringly. To be sure, most counters are likely to get heat at one point or another in their playing careers, especially if they don't camouflage their play. But most of the time counters are not bothered by casino personnel. If casinos actually gave heat to all the card counters at their tables, they would lose hundreds of good (losing) customers every busy night.

I'm not trying to give the impression that dealers and pit bosses are talented con artists, who can act like they are afraid of card counters, while knowing most counters are losers. Lower level casino employees, such as dealers and pit bosses, know very little about card counting. Even those few who are trained to count cards, in order to recognize counters, often believe that card counters pose a real threat to their profits. There is no reason for the upper management of the casinos to educate dealers and pit bosses about the realities of card counting. Dealers and pit bosses, like many in the gambling subculture, are often highly superstitious, and ignorant of the mathematics of any of the casinos' games. Casino executives do not discourage unwarranted fears, superstitions, or ignorance in their floor personnel. Counters love to share stories about superstitious pit bosses. To most counters, casino management is "dumb". This reminds me of Lenny Bruce's "Religions, Inc." bit, where the fire-and-brimstone preacher is accused of being dumb. "Yeah, I'm a big dummy," he responds to his detractors. "I've got two Lincoln Continentals, that's how damn dumb I am!"

Blackjack as a Sport

People enjoy taking risks. Gambling, of any type, is a rush. Casino blackjack combines this run for the money with a competitive angle, a game of wit and subterfuge. Every turn of the cards is a cliff-hanger. Blackjack has become popular, not because people think they can get rich playing it, but because it has been shown to be a game of skill. Card counting is more interesting than picking a number on a roulette wheel, more challenging than pulling the handle of a slot machine. Many people who play blackjack have no interest in any of the other casino games. Most do not seriously dream of getting rich at the blackjack tables. Like myself, they are often people who had never entered a casino until they'd discovered that one of the games could be beaten by applying an intelligent, systematic strategy. It's unfortunate that so many systems sellers, authors and publishers believe that people must be promised great wealth to interest them in casino blackjack.

You don't have to make a hundred thousand dollars to make this game exciting. If you practice hard, and you are dedicated, you'll almost definitely come out ahead of the game in the long run. But why risk your life savings? What's wrong with making a few hundred bucks here, a few hundred bucks there? For most people, the reward is in the *play*, not the pay.

I like to compare card counting with the oriental martial arts. The immediate analogy which comes to mind is between the Aikido master, who may be smaller and less powerful than his opponent, and the card counter, who is likewise the underdog. Yet the master of Aikido conquers his seemingly more powerful opponent through superb balance, exploiting his opponent's weaknesses, and keeping one step ahead of the fight at all times. In essence, this is how a card counter makes money at the blackjack tables.

A couple of years ago I realized that the fastest way to make the most money from card counting would be to open my own casino. Unfortunately, my $300 savings was not sufficient seed capital for this venture. I did the next best thing—I started selling inside information about card counting to other players. I set up a network of professional players, mathematicians, and computer experts to share facts, experiences, and research, and started publishing a quarterly technical journal. Yet, I never stopped playing the game for fun, mostly for nickel ($5) chips.

To play the stock market or the commodities market takes a lot of money. Many people can't afford to buy into these games. It doesn't take nearly so much money to play blackjack. This is one of the reasons it's so popular. You can watch your money go up and down right before your eyes. It's a combination of Friday night poker, chess, and cops-and-robbers. If you're good, you'll win more often than you'll lose. Your vacations may end up paying for themselves.

But I wouldn't advise any neophyte blackjack enthusiast to quit work and hock his car in order to stake his million-dollar fantasy. If, as you practice basic strategy, you feel the urge to dream about piloting your own airplane to your private island in the Caribbean, remember that card counting isn't a hobby, it's a religion. My people, all you really have to do to win is send me a hundred bucks, a measley sum compared to the riches that await you at the green felt tables. I'll personally put in a good word for you with that Great Pit Boss in the Sky.

> *"I see a world where the trees, the forests, the mountains—yes, and the Grand Canyon itself—will be laced in flashing Vegas neon! And spelled out in lights, stretched across the Rocky Mountains, for as far as the eye can see, will be the message of the First Church of Blackjack to the World: 'Welcome, My People, to Blackjack Heaven!'"*

♣♦♠♥

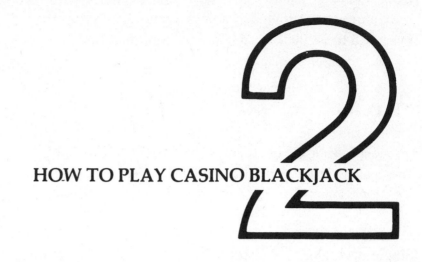

HOW TO PLAY CASINO BLACKJACK

Before you attempt to learn any winning strategy, it's important that you familiarize yourself with the game of blackjack, as played in a casino, including all rules, procedures, and options.

Blackjack is one of the easiest casino games to play. After an hour of practice with a deck of cards, following the procedures in this chapter, you will find that you could comfortably play blackjack in a casino. You cannot *beat* the game this easily, but the rules and procedures are simple enough that anyone could understand and *play* the game with this small amount of practice.

The Table

This is how a casino blackjack table appears from the top:

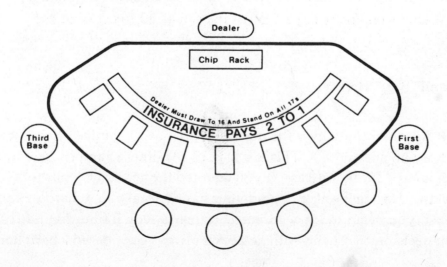

The large circles represent the seats, which can accommodate from one to seven players. The small rectangles represent the marked areas on the table top where players place their bets. There is usually a "limit" sign posted on the table, which states the minimum and maximum bets allowed. Table minimums may run from $1 to $100, and maximums may run from $25 to $4,000. $2, $3, and $5 minimum tables are most common.

The Deal

The cards are dealt from the dealer's left to right, thus the designation of the first seat on the dealer's left as "first base". The last seat is referred to as "third base".

Blackjack was originally dealt from a single 52-card deck of standard playing cards. Single-deck games are still available in many Nevada casinos, but many casinos also shuffle together anywhere from two to eight decks. If more than two decks are used, the shuffled cards are placed into a specially designed box on the table called a "shoe", which facilitates the dealing.

The object of the game is to get a "total" of 21, or as close to it as possible without going over ("busting"). Players do not play against each other, but only against the dealer, who follows house rules in playing his hand. Whoever scores closer to 21 wins. If player and dealer tie, it is called a "push", and neither wins.

In totaling the hands, cards valued 2, 3, 4, 5, 6, 7, 8 and 9 count exactly at their face value, i.e., a deuce counts 2. Cards valued 10, Jack, Queen and King each count 10 points. The ace may count as either 1 or 11, whichever the player prefers.

It makes no difference whether a card is a spade, a heart, a diamond, or a club. Any two-card hand which consists of one ace and one ten-valued card, is called a "Blackjack" or a "natural", and is an automatic win, paid off at the rate of $3 to every $2 bet.

"Hard" Hands and "Soft" Hands

Definition: Any hand in which the ace is counted as 11 *without busting* is a *soft* hand. Example: You hold an ace and a 7. This is a *soft* 18. Another example: You hold an ace, a 9, and an 8. This is a *hard* 18. In this case, if you counted the ace as 11, your total would be 28, a bust. It's important that you be able to read your hand's total value, hard or soft, quickly and effortlessly. When you begin to learn winning strategies, you'll find that hard and soft hands require different decisions. (A hand with no aces is always considered a hard hand.)

The Play of the Hands

The dealer shuffles the deck or decks, then offers the shuffled cards to be cut by a player. Sometimes, especially in single-deck games, this cut is done exactly as in poker or any other home card game. The cards are set on the table by the dealer, and a player simply cuts a portion of the cards from the top of the deck onto the table. Sometimes, a "cut card" is used. This is a specially colored card which the player might insert into the deck to indicate the cut, or he might perform a standard cut onto the cut card which the dealer would have placed beside the deck. Cut cards are always used in shoe games.

After the cut, the dealer "burns" a card. This means that he removes the top card from play by placing it either upside down on the bottom of the deck in a single-deck game, or in the "discard tray" in a multi-deck shoe game.

Before any cards are dealt, all bets must be placed. Each player has a betting spot on the table on which his wager is made. The dealer then deals two cards to each player. The players' cards may be dealt face up or face down, depending on the casino. Since players do not play against each other, but only against the dealer, and since the dealer must play his hand according to pre-set house rules regardless of what any player holds, it makes no difference if the players' hands are dealt face up or face down. If the players' cards are dealt face up, players are not allowed to touch their cards. If dealt face down, each player must pick up his two cards in order to see his hand and make his playing decisions.

Insurance

Prior to playing any hands, if the dealer's up card is an ace, he will ask: "Insurance?" This means that the dealer is offering a side-bet that he has a natural. There is a specially marked area on the table for insurance bets. If the player is willing to bet that the dealer does, in fact, have a ten-valued card in the hole, for a blackjack, the player places an amount of money equal to up to one-half his original bet in the insurance space. Thus, if a player has $10 bet on the hand, he may make an insurance bet of up to $5, but no more. After all insurance bets are placed, the dealer peeks at his hole card. If he has a natural, he immediately turns it up and proceeds to pay off insurance bets, and to collect all original wagers placed by the players. Insurance bets are paid at the rate of 2 to 1. A player with a $10 original bet, and a $5 insurance bet, would lose his original $10, since the dealer's natural is an automatic win, but would be paid $10 for his $5 insurance bet. Thus, the player breaks even. If the player and dealer *both* hold a natural, this hand is a push, and no money is exchanged. If an insurance bet had been placed, however, the insurance bet would still be paid off at the rate of 2 to 1.

If the dealer does not have a natural, all insurance bets are immediately collected by the dealer, and the play of the hands resumes, starting with the first base player and working clockwise.

Hitting

Assuming the player does not have a natural, which is an automatic win, the player's most common decision is whether to Hit or Stand. Hitting is taking another card. Example: A player holds a 5 and an 8 for a total of 13. He decides to try to get a total closer to 21, so he *signals* the dealer for a hit. In a face-up game (i.e., a game in which all players' cards are dealt face up, hence, players are not allowed to touch their cards), the player signals for a hit by scratching the table-top with his finger. In a face-down game where the player must pick up his first two cards, the player signals for a hit by scratching on the table-top with the edge of his cards. The dealer then deals the player another card face-up on the table. The player may not touch this or any subsequent cards dealt to him. Let's say this card is a deuce. The player may now decide to stand (not take any more cards) or hit again. The player may hit as many times as he chooses, so long as his total does not exceed 21.

Standing

A player signals he wants to stand by either waving his hand sideways, palm down in a face-up game, or by sliding his original two cards face-down beneath his wager, in a face-down game.

Busting

If, after a hit, a player's hand totals more than 21, he immediately lays his original two cards face up on the table. The dealer will collect the player's wager. In a face-up game, the player need do nothing as the dealer will see the bust, sometimes remarking, "too many", as he collects the bet.

Doubling Down

A player may also elect to double-down on his first two cards. This means that the player doubles the size of his bet, and that he receives one and only one hit card. In the face-up game, this is signaled simply by placing an amount of money on the table equal to the amount of his original bet. In the face-down game, the player places his original two cards face up on the table behind his bet, then places an amount of money equal to his original bet beside it in his betting spot. A casino may have restrictions on when a player may double down. Some allow doubling down on *any* two original cards. Some restrict the doubling down option to hard totals of 9, 10, and 11 only, some to 10 and 11 only, and some to 11 only. There are even a few casinos that allow doubling down on *more* than two cards, but this rule variation is rare.

Splitting Pairs

If a player holds two cards of the same value, he may split the pair into two separate hands. For example, let's say you are dealt two 8's. You do not have to play this as a single hand totaling 16. By placing an amount of money equal to your original bet on the table, you may play each 8 as a separate hand. Again, in the face-up game, you do not touch the cards, but simply take this option by putting your money on the table. In the face-down game, you separate each of your cards face-up on the table, and add the bet for the second hand beside one of the cards. When you split aces, most casinos do not allow more than *one* additional card on each ace. Likewise, most casinos allow non-ace pairs to be *resplit* as many times as you want. If, for instance, you split a pair of 8's, and received another 8 on one of the hands, most casinos would allow you to resplit and play a third hand. Usually, split aces may *not* be resplit. If you receive a ten on one of your split aces, this hand counts as 21, but is *not* a blackjack. You will not be paid 3 to 2. The dealer will complete his hand, and if he totals 21 also, it is a push. Most casinos allow you to split *any* ten-valued cards. For instance, you may split a Jack and a King. Some casinos, however, require that only *identical* ten-valued cards, such as two Kings, may be split. As with split aces, if you split tens and draw an ace on one of them, it is not counted as a blackjack. Unless informed otherwise, assume the standard pair-splitting rules: Any pair may be split. Any pair, except aces, may be resplit. Split aces receive only one card each.

There are also some casinos which allow you to Double Down after splitting. For instance, you split a pair of 8's, and on one of the hands you are dealt a 3 for a total of 11. Some casinos will allow you to Double Down on this hand if you so desire.

Surrender

In a few casinos, the player may Surrender his first two cards and lose only half his bet. This means that the hand will not be played out. The dealer will collect the player's cards and exactly one half the amount the player had wagered. The other half of the wager is returned to the player. Surrender is *not* allowed if the dealer has a natural, in which case the player loses his whole bet. At one time, the Atlantic City casinos did allow players to surrender *before* the dealer checked for a natural. This rule is called *Early Surrender*. It is not currently available at any U.S. casino. (The original surrender rule is now often referred to as *Late Surrender*.)

No Hole Card

In some casinos, notably in Atlantic City, the dealer does not check his hole card until after all the players complete their hands. This means that the dealer may ultimately get a natural and beat the table. If a player had doubled down or split a pair, he would lose only his *original* bet, if he were playing in any casino in this country. The *European* no hole card rule is different. In most European casinos, if the player doubles down or splits a pair, he will lose *all* if the dealer gets a natural.

The Dealer's Hand

The dealer completes his own hand only after all players have completed their hands. The dealer has *no* options. He is not allowed to double down or split any pair. He is not allowed to surrender. He *must* hit any hand which totals less than 17 and stand on any hand which totals 17 or more. The only exception to this is that some casinos require the dealer to hit a soft 17. In these casinos, the dealer stands on hard 17 or over, and soft 18 or over. In no casino does the dealer have any choice about how to play his hand. He must follow house rules. If, for instance, you are playing in a face-up game, and the dealer sees that you have stood on a total of 15, when his hand totals 16, he does *not* win. He *must* hit his hand when his total is less than 17.

This covers all of the rules of standard casino blackjack. There are also some rare rules you may encounter in this country which do not affect the game significantly. A few casinos offer small "Bonuses" for certain player hands, such as a holding of 6, 7 and 8 in the same suit. Some casinos offer a blackjack variation called "Double Exposure" in which *both* of the dealer's first two cards are dealt face up, *but* the dealer wins all ties. This is a relatively new game introduced in the past few years, requiring a different strategy from standard blackjack and is not covered in this book. This game is available at only a few Nevada casinos.

If you have never played blackjack in a casino, then you should spend an hour playing with a friend, or just by yourself, till you feel comfortable with the game. Refer to each section of this chapter as you play, to be sure you understand all of the rules and procedures. Use coins or poker chips to settle bets. Don't worry about minor details, such as the precise method of "scratching" for a hit. You'll understand the correct signals within a few minutes of observation in a casino. If you're not quite sure of some signal or rule variations when you are playing in a casino, the dealer will be happy to explain if you ask. There is no harm in appearing unknowledgeable in a casino. Casinos cater to tourists, and explaining the procedures of the games is a part of their job.

♣♦♠♥

BASIC STRATEGY

Once you understand how to play blackjack, you can begin to learn how to play without losing money. If you make your decisions by playing your hunches, you will lose in the long run. There is only one correct decision for any given play, and that decision is based strictly on mathematics. Whether or not you should hit or stand depends on what the laws of probability predict to be your expectations for these possibilities. Mathematicians, using high speed computers, have analyzed each and every possible hand you might hold vs. every possible dealer up card.

Definition: *Basic Strategy* is the optimum way to play your hands if you are *not* counting cards. Depending on the rules and the number of decks in use, basic strategy will usually cut the house edge to no more than ½% over the player. This makes blackjack the least disadvantageous game in the casino, even if you are not a card counter.

To explain why the various basic strategy decisions are best would require extensive mathematical proof. Unless you understand the math, and have a high speed computer to work it out, you'll have to accept basic strategy on faith. There is an underlying logic to basic strategy, however, which can be understood by anyone who understands the rules of blackjack.

Why Basic Strategy Works

In a 52-card deck, there are 16 ten-valued cards: four 10's, four Jacks, four Queens, and four Kings. (For purposes of simplification, when I refer to a card as a "ten" or "X", it is understood to mean any 10, Jack, Queen, or King.) Every other denomination has only four cards, one of each suit. You are four times more likely to pull a ten out of the deck than, say, a deuce. Likewise, the dealer's hole card is four times more likely to be a ten than a five. If you take a hit, your hit card is four times more likely to be a ten than an eight.

Always assume the dealer's hole card is a ten. If his up card is a 7, 8, 9 or X, you would assume the dealer has a "pat" hand, i.e., he will not have to take a hit card. Thus, if you were holding a "stiff", any hand totaling 12 through 16, you would hit.

If the dealer's up card is 2, 3, 4, 5 or 6, you would assume that *he* was stiff, and would therefore have to take a hit. If you were holding a stiff hand, you would usually stand in this circumstance, and let the dealer take the chance of busting.

Similarly, if the dealer's up card indicates he may be stiff, you would find it more advantageous to double down or to split pairs, thereby getting more money onto the table when the dealer has a high chance of busting.

Basic strategy says *never take insurance*. Why? Because when you take insurance, you are simply making a bet that the dealer has a ten in the hole. Insurance pays 2 to 1. However, there is fewer than one ten for every two non-tens in a deck of cards. In the long run, you'll lose more money on insurance than you'll win.

Using the Basic Strategy Chart

Do not attempt to learn all aspects of basic strategy at once. Regardless of the number of decks or rule variations, basic strategy for any game is essentially the same. Since few casinos offer the late surrender option, you need not learn this unless you intend to play in those casinos. Since virtually no casinos offer the early surrender option, the basic strategy for this rule variation is at present of academic interest only. Should you encounter a casino which offers this option, you will find the basic strategy for early surrender in the Appendix. If you will most likely be playing in Reno, there is no use learning the soft doubling down strategies, nor any hard doubling down strategies, other than for player totals of 10 and 11. In most Northern Nevada casinos, you are only allowed to double down on 10 and 11.

The basic strategy chart presented here is a "composite" basic strategy, good for any set of rules, and any number of decks. Actually, as these conditions change, some of the basic strategy decisions also change. Usually these changes are for borderline decisions, and do not significantly change your expectation. I know a number of high stakes pros who know only one basic strategy, and ignore the fine changes caused by rule variations and the number of decks in play. In the Appendix, a complete basic strategy, including all the changes according to rule and deck variations is presented. This is for advanced players, or for players who expect to do most of their playing under the same set of rules and conditions, and who would like to play accurately. For now, I advise learning this composite basic strategy which may be all you will ever need.

Two pair splitting tables are presented here. The first one assumes that you are *not* allowed to double down after splitting a pair. In most Nevada casinos, this is the rule. In a few Las Vegas casinos, and all Atlantic City casinos, players *are* allowed to double down after pair splits. If you plan to play primarily in Atlantic City, study the second table. Note that there are only a few differences between these tables. If you'll be playing in both Nevada and Atlantic City, just learn the first table, then brush up on the differences prior to your trips. In any case, you need to study and learn only one of the two pair splitting tables.

COMPOSITE BASIC STRATEGY

(Good for any set of rules or number of decks)

S = STAND
D = DOUBLE DOWN
$ = SPLIT
¢ = SURRENDER

STAND

	2	3	4	5	6	7	8	9	X	A
17+	S	S	S	S	S	S	S	S	S	S
16	S	S	S	S	S					
15	S	S	S	S	S					
14	S	S	S	S	S					
13	S	S	S	S	S					
12			S	S	S					
A8	S	S	S	S	S	S	S	S	S	S
A7	S	S	S	S	S	S	S			
A6										

DOUBLE DOWN

	2	3	4	5	6	7	8	9	X	A
11	D	D	D	D	D	D	D	D	D	D
10	D	D	D	D	D	D	D	D		
9		D	D	D	D					

SOFT

	2	3	4	5	6	7	8	9	X	A
A7		D	D	D	D					
A6		D	D	D	D					
A5			D	D	D					
A4			D	D	D					
A3				D	D					
A2				D	D					

PAIR SPLITS

	2	3	4	5	6	7	8	9	X	A
AA	$	$	$	$	$	$	$	$	$	$
99	$	$	$	$	$		$	$		
88	$	$	$	$	$	$	$	$	$	$
77	$	$	$	$	$	$				
66		$	$	$	$					
33			$	$	$	$				
22			$	$	$	$				

WITH DOUBLE AFTER SPLITS

	2	3	4	5	6	7	8	9	X	A
AA	$	$	$	$	$	$	$	$	$	$
99	$	$	$	$	$		$	$		
88	$	$	$	$	$	$	$	$	$	$
77	$	$	$	$	$	$				
66	$	$	$	$	$					
44				$	$					
33	$	$	$	$	$	$				
22	$	$	$	$	$	$				

SURRENDER

	2	3	4	5	6	7	8	9	X	A
16								¢	¢	¢

INSURANCE

NEVER!

The charts are straightforward. The player's hands are listed vertically down the left side. The dealer's up cards are listed horizontally along the top. Thus, if you hold a hand totaling 14 vs. a dealer 6, you can see the basic strategy decision is "S", or Stand. With a total of 14 vs. a dealer 7, since "S" is not indicated, you would hit. *Note:* If your total of 14 is comprised of a pair of 7's, you must consult the pair splitting chart *first*. You can see that with a pair of 7's vs. either a dealer 6 or 7, you would split ($) your 7's.

Order of Decisions

Use the basic strategy chart in this order:

1. If surrender (¢) is allowed ("early" or "late"), this takes priority over any other decision. If basic strategy calls for surrender, throw in the hand.

2. If you have a pair, determine whether or not basic strategy calls for a split.

3. If you have a possible "Double Down" hand, this play takes priority over hitting or standing. For instance, in Las Vegas and Atlantic City, you may double down on any two cards. Thus, with a holding of A7 (soft 18) vs. a dealer 5, your basic strategy play, as per the chart, is to double down. In Northern Nevada, where you may double down on 10 or 11 only, your correct play would be to stand.

4. After determining that you do not want to surrender, split a pair, or double down, consult the "Stand" chart. Always hit a hard total of 11 or below. Always stand on a hard total of 17 or higher. For all "stiff" hands, hard 12 through 16, consult the basic strategy chart. Always hit soft 17 (A6) or below. Always stand on soft 19 (A8) or higher. With a soft 18 (A7), consult the chart.

How to Practice Basic Strategy

1. *Study the Charts*

Any professional card counter could easily and quickly reproduce from memory a set of basic strategy charts. Study the charts one section at a time. Start with the hard Stand decisions. Look at the chart. Observe the pattern of the decisions as they appear in the chart, close your eyes and visualize this pattern. Study the chart once more, then get out your pencil and paper. Reproduce the hard Stand chart. Do this for each section of the chart separately—hard Stand, soft Stand, hard Double Down, soft Double Down, Pair Splits, and Surrender. Do this until you have mastered the charts.

2. *Practice with Cards*

Place an ace face up on a table to represent the dealer's up card. Shuffle the rest of the cards, then deal two cards face up to yourself. Do not deal the dealer a down card. Look at your two cards and the dealer's ace and make your basic strategy decision. Check the chart to see if you are correct. Do *not* complete your hand. If the decision is "hit", don't bother to take the hit card. After you've made and double-checked your decision, deal another two cards to yourself. Don't bother to pick up your first hand. Just drop your next, and all subsequent, cards face up on top of the last cards dealt. Go through the entire deck (25 hands), then change the dealer's up card to a deuce, then to a 3, 4, 5, etc. You should be able to run through a full deck of player hands for all ten dealer up cards in less than half an hour once you are able to make your decisions without consulting the charts. Every decision should be instantaneous when you are proficient. Strive for perfection. If you have the slightest doubt about any decision, consult the chart.

To practice your pair split decisions, which occur less frequently than other decisions, reverse the above exercise. Deal yourself a pair of aces, then run through the deck changing only the dealer's up card. Then give yourself a pair of deuces, etc. Don't waste time with any exercise you don't need. Your basic strategy for splitting aces, for instance, is *always* to split them. You don't need to run through a whole deck of dealer up cards every day to practice this decision. Likewise, basic strategy tells you *always* to split 8's, and *never* to split 4's, 5's, or 10's. You will learn these decisions quickly. Most of your study and practice for pair-splitting decisions should go toward learning when to split 2's, 3's, 6's, 7's, and 9's.

If you learn to play basic strategy, without counting cards, most casinos will have only a ½ % edge over you. In single-deck Las Vegas games, you will be playing even with the house. If you play blackjack for high stakes, it is wise to learn basic strategy, even if you are not inclined to count cards. Playing basic strategy accurately will greatly cut your losses.

Simplified Basic Strategy

If you do not intend to learn accurate basic strategy, you can cut the house edge to about 1% by playing an approximate basic strategy. Follow these rules:

1. Never take insurance.

2. If the dealer's up card is 7, 8, 9, X or A, hit until you get to hard 17 or more.

3. If the dealer's up card is 2, 3, 4, 5, or 6, stand on all your stiffs; hard 12 through 16.

4. Hit all soft hands of soft 17 (A6) or below.

5. Stand on soft 18 (A7) or higher.

6. Double down on 10 and 11 vs. any dealer up card from 2 through 9.

7. Always split aces and 8's.

8. Never split 4's, 5's, or 10's.

9. Split all other pairs, 2's, 3's, 6's, 7's, and 9's vs. any dealer up card of 4, 5 or 6.

10. Surrender 16 vs. 9, X, or A.

If you intend to learn to count cards, first learn to play accurate basic strategy. Once you know basic strategy, your decisions will become automatic. Assuming you brush up on your charts occasionally, you will not have to continue practicing basic strategy. Even when you are counting cards, you will play basic strategy on 4 out of 5 hands. Basic strategy is your single most powerful weapon.

♣♦♠♥

HOW MUCH MONEY DO YOU NEED?

Allowing for Normal Fluctuation

Before you get into the techniques of card counting, you should understand some of the practical considerations of bankrolling your play. Essentially, what you are up against is *fluctuation*. When you count cards, sometimes you will win, and sometimes you will lose. In the short run, anything can happen. Although the casinos enjoy a large edge on their slot machines, some slot players on some days win more than they lose. This is why people return to the slots. If all slot players lost every time they played, no one would play.

Let's stick with blackjack, though. Assume you learn to play basic strategy, so that you nearly eliminate the house edge. *How much* can you win or lose due to normal fluctuation?

Start by considering all of your bets to be of equal size. Rather than assigning some $ value, let's say you are betting *one unit* on each hand. We will assume you are in a single-deck Las Vegas Strip game, playing perfect basic strategy, so that for all intents and purposes, the game is dead even. Over the long run, you'd expect to win nothing and lose nothing. It's like flipping a coin.

Of course, if you try flipping a coin a thousand times, and recording the results, you'd be highly unlikely to come up with exactly 500 wins and 500 losses. There are precise mathematical formulas for predicting the limits of normal fluctuation. With an introductory course in probability and statistics, you would know how to make such estimations. For most players, this math background is unnecessary. All you need is a practical guide describing the best and worst you might expect due to normal fluctuation.

In one hour of play, or about a hundred hands, in a dead even game, you will not usually be ahead or behind by more than 20 units. On rare occasions, however, you may expect to be ahead or behind by as many as 35 units after a single hour.

If you play off and on over a period of a few days—about a thousand hands, you will not usually be ahead or behind by more than 75 units. On rare occasions you might be ahead or behind by 120 units after a few days of play. These estimates of fluctuation assume you are betting only *one unit* on each hand.

Your Bankroll

So, how big is your playing bankroll? Definition: *Bankroll*: the amount of money you can afford to lose, over a specified period of time. Ask yourself, "How much can I afford to lose this weekend, painlessly?" That is the size of your bankroll for this weekend. How big of a unit can you afford to play with? Divide your weekend bankroll by 120. That is your safe betting unit. If you intend to play longer than one weekend, and especially if you are serious about card counting for profit, you should use a more sophisticated method of bet-sizing, called *proportional* bet-sizing.

When you first start to play blackjack in a casino environment, regardless of whether you are playing basic strategy only or attempting to count cards, your first sessions must be viewed as *practice* sessions. There are a number of betting guidelines you can follow when initially practicing in casinos, which will prepare you for the more difficult techniques of bet-sizing when you are counting cards and playing "for real". These guidelines do *not* comprise a winning system, but are merely a practice exercise which will train you to size your bets in proportion to your bankroll. Later, when you are counting cards, you will use these same techniques in conjunction with other methods.

Your bankroll, in units, must be able to withstand the short run fluctuations. If you have a total of about $500 "play money", you would be courting disaster if you started making $25 bets. $500 would represent only 20 units of $25 each, and you could easily lose your whole stake in less than an hour. Making $10 bets would be safer, since you would have 50 units to play with, but this could also be lost in a relatively short run of hands just due to fluctuation. With $5 bets, or one hundred units, you'd be unlikely to lose your whole bankroll in a single weekend of play, though even this would be possible.

The first step to proportional bet-sizing is to constantly reassess the size of your bankroll, and, based on this reassessment, to systematically change the size of your betting unit. Here's how to do it:

Proportional Bet-Sizing for a Weekend (1,000 Hands):

First, divide your total bankroll into one hundred units. Let's assume you have $500, so you have one hundred $5 units. Here's how to handle a losing streak:

If you lose twenty units, or $100, quit play and reassess your bankroll. Since you now have only $400, you divide this into one hundred units, and your new unit becomes $4. Play at this level until you lose *25* units, which is another $100 loss (or one fifth of your *original* $500 bankroll).

Your bankroll would now be $300, and your betting unit would become $3. Play at this level until you lose another $100 (about 33 units), at which point your bankroll would be only $200. As per the above, your unit of play would now become $2. If you lost 50 of these units, you would still have $100 left. At this point, you could cut back to $1, if possible, or just continue betting with $2 units until you lost all of your money. A losing streak of this magnitude would be highly unlikely to occur in only a few days of play, since you have actually divided your $500 bankroll into 178 units (20 + 25 + 33 + 50 + 50).

Of course, it's pessimistic to assume you are going to lose and lose and keep losing. There is an equal chance that you'll go on an equivalent winning streak. In this circumstance, each time you add $100 to your bankroll, you may add $1 to your betting unit.

None of this will have any effect on the fact that over the long run, your expectation will be to break even, assuming you're playing in an even game. The purpose of the above betting method is primarily to train you to constantly monitor bankroll size, and to keep you in the game longer when you hit a losing streak. It will not give you any long run advantage.

If your starting bankroll is larger than $500, you may adjust the unit size proportionately, to see what kind of fluctuations you might expect, but I would not advise playing for high stakes unless you have a decided edge. Keep in mind also that you will be playing with casino chips, which come in specific denominations, and that your smallest betting unit will be limited to the table minimum bet allowed where you are playing. Most U.S. casinos have $25, $5, $2 and $1 chips. Many casinos have $100 and/or $3 chips, and some have $2.50 chips (used for paying off odd blackjacks). Some Nevada casinos have tables with $1 minimums, but most casinos now require $2 or $3 minimum bets. If you are practicing in a casino where you must place $3 minimum bets, and your starting bankroll is $500, you would be wise to start out with a $3 betting unit, and never vary from this, unless you came ahead a few hundred dollars.

If your starting bankroll is less than $500, or if $500 represents a significant amount of money to you, play only table minimum bets when practicing. Be aware that you must view this money as "play money", as you could conceivably lose it all, due to normal fluctuation.

If the house has a slight edge (½% to 1%) due to unfavorable rules, number of decks, or your own less than perfect basic strategy, you may still use the above guidelines for sizing your bets. Be aware that when the house has an edge, your bankroll will inevitably be depleted over the long run. In the short run, anything can happen. If *you* have a slight edge, due to card counting and expert play, you may likewise follow the above practice guidelines, though over the long run, your bankroll should steadily increase.

For card counters, and especially for high stakes players, bet-sizing is more complex than the simple guidelines presented here. We will get into bet-sizing for advanced players in Chapter Nine of this book, since these techniques will not concern you until you have acquired considerable skill and experience.

The betting guidelines in this chapter are presented for beginners to use when practicing at low stakes. If you have a $50,000 bankroll, you would be ill-advised to follow the guidelines in this chapter, i.e., divide this bankroll into 100 units of $500 each, in a break-even (or negative-edge) game, just so you could practice basic strategy. Why chance losing 20 to 30 thousand dollars in a short period of play just for practice? Practice at low stakes, then use your big money to bankroll your play when you know what you're doing.

Note that fluctuation is dependent on two factors: the size of your betting unit, and the number of hands you play. Also note that it is not a direct multiple of the number of hands you play. For instance, although you could easily lose 25 units after a hundred bets of one unit each, you would never expect to lose 250 units after a thousand bets of one unit each, due to normal fluctuation. As mentioned above, after a thousand bets of one unit each, you would never expect to lose more than about 120 units, due to normal fluctuation, unless you are making some gross playing errors, or the game you are playing in is far from being an even game.

Proportional Bet-Sizing for a Month (10,000 Hands)

You could lose more than 120 units in an even game, due to normal fluctuation, if you played more than 1,000 hands. For instance, let's say you are planning an extended session of playing blackjack during a 3- or 4-week trip, and you expect to play for a total of about 100 hours, or about 10,000 hands. After playing this many hands, you would not usually be ahead or behind by more than 250 units, but on rare occasions, you might find yourself ahead or behind by as many as 400 units, due to normal fluctuation (and a slight house edge).

For this reason, if your total playing bankroll is only a few thousand dollars or less, you could conceivably lose it all, due to normal fluctuation, even if you become an expert card counter. You could ultimately be a victim of the table minimum bets. If, as your losing streak continued, you were allowed to cut back to bets of $1, then 50¢, 25¢, etc., you would never lose all of your money. In the long run, your losing streak would end, and your edge over the house would begin to pay off. But casinos do set minimum betting requirements. If your bankroll is insufficient, you should not be making any bets at all.

Most players, of course, will not experience inordinate losing streaks, and some will even experience inordinate winning streaks. Fluctuation is probably the leading deterrent to card counting. Most beginning counters overbet their bankrolls. Those with negative fluctuations give up. Those with positive fluctuations usually increase the size of their bets proportionately, thus continuing to overbet their bankrolls, until their first big negative swing wipes them out.

Proportional bet-sizing for a 3- or 4-week period of play (10,000 hands), works exactly the same as proportional bet-sizing for a weekend. The only difference is that you should start by dividing your total bankroll by 250, instead of 100, in order to determine your betting unit. In other words, to make $5 bets, you should have a bankroll of $1,250. Cut back to a $4 betting unit if your bankroll hits $1,000; $3 units if you fall to $750, etc.

As you can see, the greater the number of hands you will be playing, the larger your bankroll must be to ensure your continuance in the game—even when the game is a break even proposition. In fact, the only way to get around this is to get the edge in *your* favor. In the long run, your edge will assure you that your expected winnings will be greater than the possible negative fluctuations.

To last in this game, you must have sufficient money. You must size your bets in proportion to your bankroll. You must reassess your bankroll frequently. You must *never chase losses* by increasing your bet size to win back money you've lost. If you follow these guidelines, you will last forever at the tables. If you persevere, and acquire skill, you're on your way to winning.

♣♦♠♥

THE RED SEVEN COUNT

Balanced Systems

Most professional level card counting systems are *balanced point-count* systems. Plus and minus point values are assigned to the various cards, and as these cards are seen, the player adds the point values in his head to his *running count*. Once learned, this aspect of card counting becomes automatic and easy. The count system is said to be "balanced" because there are an equal number of "plus" and "minus" point values. The sum of all these plus and minus values is zero. The difficulty of playing a balanced point-count system comes when attempting to use the running count for betting and strategy decisions. First, the running count must be converted to a *true count* (see Chapter Eight for an in-depth explanation of true count). Second, the player must have memorized, and be able to apply, the correct *strategy index number* for each decision.

These two technical problems seem to come up again and again in my correspondence. These are excerpts from letters I've received which describe these difficulties precisely:

FROM LAS VEGAS:

"I have been counting cards for eight years now, using Revere's Point Count. I've been moderately successful at the tables, so I've stuck with this count, and believe I am as fast and accurate as any card counter in counting down a deck (or decks). Unfortunately, I still have a lot of trouble adjusting my running count for true count. In testing myself by having a friend deal, then stopping at various points for a test, my running count is always accurate. My true count estimate, which I make quickly, as I would in a casino, is often atrocious. I have been playing and practicing for years, and am afraid I simply cannot estimate deck depletion by sight. Also, I mix up multiplying and dividing sometimes when I try to figure out true count quickly in my head. Any suggestions? (I know I would be very successful at the tables if I could adjust my count more accurately.)"

AND FROM NEW YORK:

"Help! I have been practicing the Hi-Opt I count system for eight months. I learned the strategy charts with no trouble and can reproduce them completely with no mistakes on paper. But I can't use them when I play! I seem to have a mental block against correlating the right strategy number with the right decision, and when I try to do this, I lose my count! Also, I'm terrible at converting to true count. Can I make money at blackjack if I forget about the strategy tables, and just bet by my running count? I love playing blackjack, and want to win for a change. What are my chances?"

Many other such letters have convinced me that counters need an easier method of "true count" adjustment, and a simpler playing strategy. After months of mulling over the possibilities, a solution hit me—a solution so simple, yet so effective, that for the life of me I can't believe that no other blackjack expert has suggested this counting method in the twenty years since card counting was introduced.

Unbalanced Systems

In 1969, a Berkeley professor, using the pseudonym of "Jacques Noir", wrote a book called *Casino Holiday,* which came closest to this simple but effective card counting method. Later, refined versions of Noir's "unbalanced" ten count were published by other authors, though Noir was the originator. The power of this count derives from its built-in imbalance which makes it very simple to play. Tens are counted as −2, and all non-tens, including aces, are counted as +1. We call this an "unbalanced" count because the count values of the complete deck, when added together, do not equal zero. *No true count adjustments are necessary, however, because of this imbalance.*

If you count down a deck, using this count, any time your running count is +4, then the ratio of non-tens to tens is *exactly* 2 to 1. Thus, this count is a "perfect" insurance indicator *by running count*. This count has one major weakness, and that is in its betting efficiency. The ten count has a betting correlation of only 72%. Compare this to Hi-Opt I's 88%, or the Hi-Lo count's 97% correlations.

Quite a few serious players still choose this unbalanced ten count as their system, because they do not consider the difficult and frequently sloppy true count conversions necessary with balanced counts to be more than 72% accurate anyway. I agree. True count conversions are difficult for many people, who simply cannot multiply and/or divide in their heads quickly and accurately.

Why, I asked myself, is this unbalanced ten count the only unbalanced count system ever invented? Why not an unbalanced "point" count system, which would be optimized to indicate perfect betting by running count, rather than perfect insurance?

The Red Seven Count

Thus was born the "Red Seven Count". It has a betting correlation of 97% *by running count*, and an insurance correlation of 80% by running count. This count is strong enough on the major playing strategy decisions by running count, that it should probably be adopted by the vast majority of counters who seek to play with top efficiency with minimal possibility for error or mental fatigue.

Using this count, the player does not have to make any true count adjustments, nor does he have to learn any strategy indices. His play will usually be more accurate than that of most "advanced", "higher level", "multi-parameter" systems players. Why? Because the player who uses the Red Seven Count will make *very few errors*. His true count adjustments will be automatic—i.e., a function of his simple running count. Nor will this automatic adjustment be sloppily "rounded" to half-deck accuracy. This will be an *exact* adjustment to the *exact number of cards played*.

The Point Values

First learn basic strategy (Chapter Three). Most of your play, using the Red Seven Count, or any other count, will be according to basic. Next, learn to count cards by adding and subtracting the following values as the respective cards are removed from the deck:

A:	-1
10:	-1
9:	0
8:	0
Black 7:	0
Red 7:	+1
6:	+1
5:	+1
4:	+1
3:	+1
2:	+1

The one strange mechanism here, which will surprise even the most knowledgeable experts, is that I am suggesting that you count black 7's as 0, and red 7's as +1! This is the device which creates the exact imbalance necessary for this count to work. (It does not make any difference whether the red seven or the black seven is counted, so long as this precise imbalance is attained. One may even count *all* sevens as +½, or simply count *every other* seven seen as +1.)

Start by buying yourself a couple dozen decks of cards. Put one in the pocket of every one of your jackets. Put one by each telephone you use regularly. One on the kitchen table. One by each TV set. One on the dashboard of your car. Always have a deck of cards at hand. As you watch TV, talk on the phone, or enjoy your morning coffee, practice keeping your running count, using the point values for the Red Seven Count.

Practicing the Running Count

Start at 0. Turn each card over one at a time, onto the bottom of the deck, adding each card's point value to your running count. For example:

> Cards seen: 2, A, 8, 9, X, X, 5
> Point Values: +1, -1, 0, 0, -1, -1, +1
> Running Count: +1, 0, 0, 0, -1, -2, -1

By the time you get to the end of the deck, your running count should be +2. If it is not +2, then you have not counted correctly, assuming your deck contains 52 cards. If you have miscounted, turn the deck over and run through the same sequence of cards again, until your final running count is +2. Then shuffle, and go through the deck once more. Build up speed and accuracy.

When you are proficient at counting down a deck of cards in this manner, practice turning the cards over two at a time, and learn to count cards in pairs. It's faster and easier for most people to count cards in pairs. This is because many pairs cancel each other out. For instance, every time you pair a ten or ace (both -1) with a 2, 3, 4, 5, 6, or red 7 (all +1), the pair counts as zero. You will quickly learn to ignore self-canceled pairs, 8's, 9's and black 7's, since all of these are valued at 0. When you are good at counting cards in pairs, start turning them over 3 at a time. You must be accurate in your count. Speed, without accuracy, is worthless. It may take you weeks to become proficient at keeping a running count, but once you learn it, it's like telling time. You'll be able to do it automatically, and with very few errors.

As a self-test after you can count cards in pairs and groups of three, remove one card from a full deck, and turn the deck over and run through the cards, fanning them from one hand to the other, as you count. You should be able to predict the point value of the removed card accurately nine out of ten times before you're ready to try counting in a casino environment. You should be able to count down a deck in 45 seconds or less. Most pros can count down a deck in less than 30 seconds.

No matter how fast you get at counting by turning cards over yourself, you'll find counting at a casino blackjack table to be something else again. Some cards will appear as mere flashes as players throw in their hands, and dealers scoop up cards as quickly as they're turned over. Before you try counting cards in a casino while playing blackjack, spend a half-hour or so counting while watching others play. Do not sit down to play until you feel comfortable counting while watching the game.

If you plan to play in multi-deck games, practice counting down multiple decks of cards at home. Note that your final count is always 2 times the number of decks you are using.

The Red Seven Betting Strategy

Once you are good at counting, you can begin immediately to apply the Red Seven betting strategy at the tables. As explained, if all of the point values of one deck are added up, your final count will be +2. This +2 count represents your pivot. With balanced count systems, your pivot is always zero, regardless of the number of decks in play. With the Red Seven Count, your pivot is always 2 *times the number of decks in play*. In a six-deck game, your pivot is +12; with 4 decks, your pivot is +8.

Remember, when counting in a casino, that you always begin your count at 0 after a shuffle. If a shuffle occurs while some cards are still on the table, in play, immediately drop your current running count. Start at 0 and count just the cards on the table.

Any time your *running count* is at the pivot number, your advantage will have risen about 1% over your starting advantage. This 1% raise in advantage is ascertained *by running count* with a high degree of accuracy.

This pivot is a good indicator of when to raise your bet for nearly all the blackjack games available in this country. The 6-deck or 8-deck Atlantic City game, the 4-deck Las Vegas game, and the 1-deck Reno game all have a *house* advantage off the top of the deck, of about ½%. The pivot will accurately indicate by running count when the advantage has risen by about 1%, indicating when the edge has turned to *your* favor by ½%. In the single-deck Vegas game, which is just about an even money proposition off the top of the deck, the pivot indicates when you have a full 1% advantage. In the 2- and 4-deck Reno games, the pivot indicates when the advantage has turned to your favor by about ¼%. There are no commonly available games in this country, and few anywhere, where the starting advantage is more than 1% in favor of the house. Such games should be avoided by card counters. The Red Seven pivot is a highly accurate indicator of the point at which to raise your bet in most any game anywhere.

The Red Seven Playing Strategy

What about the major playing strategy decisions?

First of all, insurance is the most important strategy decision. In single-deck games, assuming you are using a moderate betting spread, insurance is almost as important as all other strategy decisions combined. Conveniently, you have a very nice insurance indicator with the Red Seven Count. In 1- and 2-deck games, you simply take insurance any time your running count is at your pivot number or higher. In games where 3 or more decks are in play, take insurance at your *pivot-plus-two*. Example: in the 6-deck Atlantic City game, your pivot is +12. Take insurance at +14. In a 4-deck game, you would insure at +10.

As for other playing decisions, there are only a few to remember. Any time you are at your pivot or higher, stand on 16 vs. 10 and stand on 12 vs. 3. (According to basic strategy you would hit both of these.) *No other strategy changes need be learned.* In single-deck games, the 16 vs. 10 decision is the second most important strategy decision for a card counter—insurance being first. The 16 vs. 10 decision is more important than all pair splitting indices combined! After you find these few strategy changes easy, there are a couple of others you can add which will increase your advantage. At your pivot plus 2, or higher, with any number of decks, stand on 12 vs.2; stand on 15 vs. 10; and double down on 10 vs. X. In multi-deck games, you will be taking advantage of about 80% of all possible gains from card counting by using this strategy. Because you will not be sloppily attempting to adjust your running count to true count on every hand, your decisions will be made with devastating accuracy. Using the Red Seven Count, you have no strategy tables to memorize! You simply have a basic strategy and a pivot strategy. Your pivot strategy indicates that you raise your bet, take insurance, and stand on 16 vs. 10 and 12 vs. 3. Only when you are capable with these strategy changes, should you learn the other three "pivot-plus-2" decisions.

There are, to be sure, weaknesses in this vastly simplified system. However, in my opinion, most card counters would be wise to ignore more difficult strategies.

Because of its combined power and simplicity, the Red Seven Count lends itself to many advanced professional approaches to beating the game of blackjack. It works excellently for table-hopping (Chapter Nine) and "one-deck Wonging" (Chapter Ten). It's also an excellent system for teams and partners. A husband/wife team, for instance, could employ a strategy where the wife counts while the husband plays. The husband need only learn basic strategy, and the pivot changes. The wife keeps the count and uses a predetermined signal to indicate the pivot. The husband would know when to raise his bet, lower his bet, and make a strategy change, according to a single signal. For advanced players, two signals could be used, one to indicate the pivot, the other to indicate the pivot-plus-2. Most team approaches to blackjack involve such complicated signal passing that teams often drill for weeks just to get the signals straight.

The Red Seven Count requires the minimum amount of memory work for a professional level system, and also relieves the player from all mathematical calculations at the table, except for the simple adding and subtracting necessary to keep the running count.

Most of the readers of this book who become card counters should stick with the Red Seven Count. It is better to play a simple system with speed and accuracy than to play a complicated system slowly, with errors and mental fatigue.

Before you decide to learn an advanced system, such as the Zen Count (Chapter Seven), there is one simple mathematical formula you should learn. I call this formula the Profit Formula.

The Profit Formula

Average Bet x Advantage x Hands Per Hour = Hourly Profit

This formula is simple, yet it provides a good approximation of what a card counter might expect to win *per hour* in the long run. Say you are making average bets of $10 with a 1% advantage over the house from card counting. You estimate you're playing about 80 hands per hour. Calculation of your potential hourly profit, then, is:

$$\$10 \times .01 \times 80 = \$8 \text{ per hour.}$$

(Note that your 1% advantage is expressed decimally as .01, for use in the formula. A 2% advantage would be .02, a 1½% advantage would be .015, etc. You might find it helpful to follow this math with a pocket calculator.)

Now, let's say you want to increase your expectation above $8 per hour. That's simple enough to do, keeping the Profit Formula in mind. Simply raise the value of one or more of the three vital factors in the formula.

Start with the first factor: *Average Bet*. Obviously, if you made an average bet of $25, your expectation would immediately rise to $20 per hour:

$$\$25 \times .01 \times 80 = \$20 \text{ per hour.}$$

That's simple, but there is a problem if you have a limited bankroll. Increasing your bet size leads to greater $ fluctuation. Although your long run win rate may rise to $20 per hour, you may never see the long run.

The next variable in the Profit Formula is *Advantage*. It's simple enough to see how to raise your expectation to $20 per hour by altering this factor; just raise your advantage to 2½%. Thus:

$$\$10 \times .025 \times 80 = \$20 \text{ per hour.}$$

This is the tactic most card counters attempt to employ. They start using an "advanced", higher level, "multi-parameter" system. They keep side counts of aces, and sometimes fives, and memorize extensive strategy tables.

Unfortunately, this tactic does not pay off as well as most counters would like to think. Even the most advanced system will rarely raise your advantage by more than ¼% to ½% over your advantage with a simple system, such as the Red Seven Count.

If you're playing with black ($100) chips, a ¼% increase may be worth the trouble, if you can play an advanced strategy with speed and accuracy. If not, you're wasting your time.

Consider a game which would net the Red Seven Count about 1%, and would net an advanced system, such as the Zen Count, about 1¼%. Whereas the Red Seven Count would win at a rate of $8 per hour, the Zen Count would win at a rate of only about $10 per hour *if you can play it* with equal speed and accuracy.

$$\$10 \times .0125 \times 80 = \$10 \text{ per hour.}$$

What if playing the Zen Count slows down your rate of play? With only 10 fewer hands per hour, the Zen Count would be raising your win rate by only 75¢ per hour. Of course, if you're making average bets of $500, this would translate to an increase of $37.50 per hour. This may be worth the effort. There are also some advanced strategies (such as "depth charging" in Chapter Ten) which *require* a more complicated counting system than the Red Seven Count.

For the average counter, however, there is little to gain from an advanced counting strategy. Most players would either slow down so much, or play so inaccurately, that they would gain nothing. Many would actually decrease their win rates.

The last factor in the Profit Formula is *Hands Per Hour*. Most blackjack authors estimate that a player gets about 75 to 100 hands per hour. Full tables may cut this down to 60 hands per hour, or even fewer if other players at the table are slow. Head-on play, when you can find it, will get you about 200 hands per hour.

Many players do not believe they can find head-on games, and when they can, they do not believe they can play 200 hands per hour. Actually, this is a pretty normal rate of play in a head-on game—if you do not waste time making your decisions.

Playing faster is more challenging, and is also an excellent cover. Dealers and pit bosses expect card counters to play thoughtfully. Dealers will often deal deeper into the deck(s) for fast players, which is a further advantage (see Chapter Six). After all, the faster you play, the more often the dealer must shuffle. If you're accomplished enough as a counter to carry on some semblance of small talk while playing your hands at a good clip, why should a dealer shuffle up?

To find head-on games, try to play at off hours. Mornings and early afternoons on weekdays are excellent times to go hunting for dealers who are standing behind empty tables twiddling their thumbs.

What, then, would these 200 hands per hour get you, assuming you're using a simple system with that $10 average bet?

$$\$10 \times .01 \times 200 = \$20 \text{ per hour.}$$

While it is either dangerous or virtually impossible to raise that original $8 per hour win rate significantly by either betting higher or employing a more "advanced" strategy, increasing your speed of play can more than double your hourly win rate.

To optimally apply the Red Seven Count, you'll need to learn much more about such factors as table conditions, betting strategies, camouflage, toking, and just about every other aspect of casino blackjack that is important to a professional player. You don't need a more complicated system. All of these other factors are covered in the following chapters.

♣♦♠♥

TABLE CONDITIONS

Many counters believe that as long as a game is called "blackjack", and is being offered by a legitimate casino, they can win by applying their counting systems. These counters do not last long—or, at least, their money doesn't last long.

Some games can be beaten by card counting, but some cannot. Table conditions make the difference. I've written two books on this subject already: *The Blackjack Formula* (RGE, 1980), and *Blackjack for Profit* (RGE, 1981). In this chapter, I will attempt to update and condense some of the most important information from these books, so that you can choose your games wisely. I advise serious players to obtain one or both of my other books on this subject. (See ordering information in the Appendix.) Judging the profit potential of blackjack games is a vast field of research unto itself, but there are definite guidelines you can follow which will help to keep you from throwing your money away in unbeatable games.

First, let's define *table conditions*. There are four distinct conditions of any blackjack game which affect profit potential for card counters:

1. *Number of decks in play*. In U.S. casinos, this may currently range from one to eight.

2. *Depth of deal prior to shuffle*. Anywhere from 20% to 90% of the cards may be dealt out between shuffles.

3. *Crowd conditions*. You may be the only player at the table, or one of as many as seven.

4. *Rules*. There are about twenty common rule variations in U.S. casinos.

The Number of Decks in Play

I'll go through these conditions one at a time. First, consider the effect of the number of decks shuffled together. All other conditions being equal, single-deck games are the most profitable for card counters. The more decks being used, the less profitable the game becomes. A single-deck Vegas Strip game, for instance, is a break even proposition for a basic strategy player. With more than one deck in play, however, the house has the edge. You can use this chart to estimate the basic strategy edge against you due to the number of decks in play:

# Decks	Starting Advantage
1	.0%
2	-.3%
3	-.4%
4, 5, 6	-.5%
7+	-.6%

Even with a hundred decks shuffled together, your Starting Advantage with Vegas Strip rules would still be about -.6%. But this does not mean all games with 7 or more decks are equal in profit potential. A large number of decks in play is devastating to the card counter's expectation. Consider an 8-deck game: if you are using the Red Seven Count, you will need a count of +16 to indicate you have a ½% edge. This will occur with extreme rarity. Regardless of what system you are using, you will almost never have a significant edge in an 8-deck game.

The Depth of the Deal

The second table condition you must consider is tied to the first: the depth of deal prior to reshuffling. In single-deck games, you cannot win significantly unless more than 50% of the cards are dealt out between shuffles. With 2-deck games, you'll want better than 60% dealt out. With 4 decks, at least 75% (3 decks) should be dealt out. You are unlikely to find any games with 6 or more decks shuffled together, where enough decks are dealt out to make for a potentially profitable game, *if you sit through every deal*. These games and most 4-deck games, are best attacked by *table-hopping*, a betting strategy which is explained in Chapter Nine.

The Number of Players at the Table

The third condition you must consider is the number of players at the table. The more hands you play per hour, the faster your win rate. If crowded tables keep you from seeing and counting all the cards played, the effect of this is the same as the effect of an inadequate depth of deal. Consider, for instance, a single-deck game where there are seven players at the table. Just two rounds will consume about 90% of the cards, which makes this game appear attractive. But remember that your second (and last) bet of each round will be made after having seen only about 45% of the cards *if you are able to see and count all cards from the first round.*

The Rules

The fourth condition you must consider is the rules of the game. There are more than 20 different rules which are commonly offered in casino blackjack. Some of these rules, notably those which offer the player more options, are favorable to the player, assuming the player applies the correct strategy. Such a rule would be, "player may surrender half his bet." Those rules which limit the player's options, such as "no soft doubling down", are disadvantageous to the player. Some rules neither limit nor offer options to the player, but alter the dealer's procedure. An example of one such rule would be "dealer hits soft seventeen." This is disadvantageous to the player. Another rule of this type would be "dealer pays $5 bonus to player hand of 6, 7, 8 of the same suit." This rule, naturally, is advantageous to the player.

In Chapter Two, the various rules were explained. In this chapter, I'll explain the effect of the rules on your expectation. You can use the information in the rule effect table to estimate your starting advantage in any game. First, account for the effect of the rule variations. You must account for all rules which vary from standard Vegas Strip rules. The Vegas Strip game assumes the following rules:

1. Dealer stands on soft 17.
2. You may double down on any 2 cards.
3. You may not double down after splitting pairs.
4. You may split any pair.
5. You may resplit any pair except aces.
6. Split aces receive only one card each.
7. No surrender.
8. Dealer either receives a hole card, *or* the player's original bet *only* is lost if the player doubles down or splits a pair and the dealer gets a blackjack.

The effect of any other rules must be accounted for in determining your starting advantage. These are the rule effects:

Rule	Effect	
No double on 11:	-.8%	
No double on 10:	-.5%	
No double on 9:	-.1%	
No double on 8, 7, 6:	0.0%	
No soft double:	-.1%	
Hits soft 17:	-.2%	
No resplitting non-aces:	0.0%	
No splitting aces:	-.2%	
No splitting non-aces:	-.2%	
No hole card (European):	-.1%	
Double after splits:	+.1%	
Double any # of cards:	+.2%	
Double on 11 only after splits:	+.1%	
Double on 10 only after splits:	+.1%	
Resplit aces:	0.0%	(Multi-deck: +.1%)
Draw to Split Aces:	+.1%	
Surrender:	0.0%	(Multi-deck: +.1%)
Early surrender:	+.6%	
Early surrender (hits soft 17)	+.7%	
2-to-1 BJ payoff:	+2.3%	

Estimating Starting Advantage

The most common games you'll find in Las Vegas are the standard Strip game vs. 4 decks, and the "downtown" Vegas game vs. 4 decks (where the dealer hits soft seventeen). To estimate your starting advantage in these games, use the tables which list the deck effects, and the rule effects. The 4-deck Vegas Strip game is easy, since there are no rule effects. Your starting advantage is simply the deck effect: -.5%. This means that if you play perfect basic strategy, over the long run, the house will win about .5% (or ½%) of the total amount of money you wager. This is 50¢ for every $100 you bet.

In the 4-deck downtown Vegas game:

4 Decks:	-.5%
Hits soft 17:	-.2%
Starting Advantage:	-.7%

In the typical Reno game, you are playing vs. a single deck, but the dealer hits soft 17, and you may double down on 10 and 11 only:

One deck:	.0%
Hits soft 17:	-.2%
No soft double:	-.1%
No double on 9:	-.1%
Starting advantage:	-.4%

In Atlantic City, there have been many changes and experiments with conditions since the "no-barring" law went into effect (September, 1982). To analyze the most common 8-deck game:

8 decks:	-.6%
No resplitting non-aces:	0.0%
Double after splits:	+.1%
Starting Advantage:	-.5%

Note that some rules are very important while others are insignificant. Note also that your starting advantage is only an initial criterion upon which to judge a game's profit potential. The 4-deck downtown Vegas game, with a starting advantage of -.7% would be potentially more profitable than the 8-deck Atlantic City game, even though the A.C. game has a better starting advantage (-.5%). This is because the edge will turn more frequently from the house to the player when there are fewer decks, assuming approximately the same proportion of cards are dealt out between shuffles.

Some Atlantic City casinos are currently experimenting with a new shuffling procedure, in which some discards are shuffled, then reinserted into the unplayed portion of the shoe. This shuffling procedure is disadvantageous to counters. You should avoid playing in games where this occurs.

One rule not mentioned in the rule effect table is *insurance*. This is because basic strategy for insurance is simply *never insure*. Whether or not a casino allows you to take insurance makes no difference to the basic strategy player. For the card counter, however, insurance is very valuable. In one- and two-deck games, it is the single most valuable strategy variation. Likewise, you may note that the effect of surrender is listed as 0.0% for single-deck games. For basic strategy players, surrender is not a significant rule. For card counters, however, it would be worth +.1% to +.2%, depending on your betting spread.

Therefore, after you figure out your starting advantage, keep in mind that this is just the starting point for a card counter. From this point, your playing and betting strategies take over. The following two chapters explain the Zen Count, an advanced, "level two" playing strategy, advisable for dedicated blackjack fanatics only. If you prefer to stick with the Red Seven Count, you may skip over Chapters Seven and Eight, and get right into Chapter Nine, "Betting Strategies".

♣♦♠♥

THE ZEN COUNT 7

This is an advanced card counting strategy for blackjack players who are willing and able to devote the time and effort necessary to mastering it. Even so, it is far simpler to learn and play than any other advanced blackjack strategy, because it has been streamlined for maximum efficiency with minimum effort. The recommended exercises for learning how to count cards are the same for the Zen Count as for the Red Seven Count, so these exercises will not be repeated here.

The Zen Count Point Values

The point values of the Zen Count are:

A :	-1
X :	-2
9 :	0
8 :	0
7 :	+1
6 :	+2
5 :	+2
4 :	+2
3 :	+1
2 :	+1

As the cards are played, the player keeps a running count of all cards seen. After a shuffle, the count always starts at 0. This is a balanced count system, so if you count down a complete deck, your final count will be 0. Because the point values are balanced, it is necessary to adjust your running count to the *True Count*, according to the number of decks. All Zen Count betting and playing strategy decisions must be made according to true count, not running count.

Definition: *True Count* is the running count divided by the number of remaining (unseen, uncounted) decks. Example: You are in a 4-deck game and one deck has been played. Your running count is +6. Your true count is +6 divided by 3 (the number of remaining decks), or +2. A few minutes later, 2 decks have been played, and your running count is -4. Your true count is -4 divided by 2 (the remaining decks), or -2. A few minutes later, 3½ decks have been played. Your running count is -3. Your true count is -3 divided by ½, or -6. (Note that we are *dividing* by ½, which is the same as *multiplying* by 2.)

The simple examples above illustrate how to adjust running count to true count. Chapter Eight deals exclusively with the subject of True Count, and explains various simplified methods and learning techniques you can use to make true count adjustments with ease.

Each true count indicates a change in your advantage by about ¼%. If you are playing in a single-deck Vegas Strip game, where your basic strategy advantage is about even off the top of the deck, a true count of +2 would indicate that you have a ½% advantage. A true count of -4 would indicate the *house* had a 1% advantage over you on the next hand dealt.

½% Advantage Chart

Naturally, you want to bet more when you have the advantage, and less (or none) when the house has the advantage. These are the approximate starting advantages of various games, rounded to ¼%, and the true count which would indicate you had a ½% advantage:

L.V. = Las Vegas

W/DAS = with double after splits rule

(HS) = Dealer hits soft 17

GAME	# DECKS	STARTING ADVANTAGE	+½% EDGE
L.V. Strip	1	0%	+ 2
L.V. Strip	2	-1/4%	+3
L.V. Strip	4	-1/2%	+4
L.V. Strip	6	-1/2%	+4
W/DAS	1	+1/4%	+1
W/DAS	2	-1/4%	+3
W/DAS	4	-1/2%	+4
W/DAS	6	-1/2%	+4
L.V. Downtown (HS)	1	-1/4%	+3
L.V. Downtown (HS)	2	-1/2%	+4
L.V. Downtown (HS)	4	-3/4%	+5
L.V. Downtown (HS)	6	-3/4%	+5
W/DAS (HS)	1	0%	+2
W/DAS (HS)	2	-1/2%	+4
W/DAS (HS)	4	-1/2%	+4
W/DAS (HS)	6	-1/2%	+4
Northern Nev.	1	-1/2%	+4
Northern Nev.	2	-3/4%	+5
Northern Nev.	4	-1%	+6
Atlantic City	6	-1/2%	+4
Atlantic City	8	-1/2%	+4

Any time your true count is below the count in the +½% column, place a minimum (or no) bet. When your true count is above the +½% number, you want to raise your bet. Chapter Nine covers special betting strategies in detail.

The Zen Count also allows you to play your cards, varying from basic strategy, with a high degree of accuracy. The strategy tables presented here will provide about 90% of all possible playing strategy gains from using the Zen Count. Use basic strategy for all decisions for which no index number is provided. To use the tables:

Stand: Stand only when your true count is equal to or higher than the number in the table.

Double: Double down only when your true count is equal to or higher than the number in the table.

Split: Split only when your true count is equal to or higher than the number in the table.

THE ZEN COUNT STRATEGY

STAND

	2	3	4	5	6	7	8	9	X	A
16								+9	0	
15	-10								+7	
14	-6	-8	-10						+13	
13	-2	-4	-5	-8	-8					
12	+7	+4	+2	-2	0					

DOUBLE DOWN

	2	3	4	5	6	7	8	9	X	A
11									-9	0
10									+7	

PAIR SPLITS

	2	3	4	5	6	7	8	9	X	A
10,10			+13	+11	+10					

INSURANCE: Take at +5 or higher true count.

This is a composite strategy table which you may use for any number of decks, and any set of rules. You will be playing with a great degree of accuracy in any game if you use the strategy decisions presented here, and follow basic strategy for all other decisions. For advanced players, there is a more complete and accurate set of strategy indices for the Zen Count in the Appendix. If you intend to play mostly single-deck games, or vs. a particular set of rules, you will find slightly more accurate strategy indices for these and other specific circumstances in the Appendix tables. ♣♦♠♥

TRUE COUNT

What is True Count?

Definition: *True Count* is an *adjusted* running count, which indicates the balance of high cards to low cards. True count is, in fact, not "true", as a *precise* indicator of your advantage. But it does reflect the *balance* of the cards, so that you may approximate your advantage, and your playing strategy.

Take a full 52-card deck. Count the point values of all the tens and aces, using the Zen Count. With 16 tens and 4 aces, the points add up to -36. If you now count all of the points of the low cards, 2's, 3's, 4's, 5's, 6's and 7's, you'll find that these add up to +36. The deck is perfectly balanced:

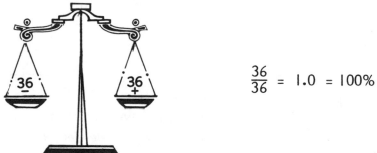

$$\frac{36}{36} = 1.0 = 100\%$$

Now, let's remove 8 tens and 2 aces from the deck. Adding up the point values of the high cards, we now get −18. Our balance looks like this:

$$\frac{18}{36} = .50 = 50\%$$

The deck is heavy in low cards and light in high cards.

There are, in fact, exactly one half (or 50%) as many high card points as low card points in the remaining deck.

If this situation occurred at a blackjack table, i.e., if 8 tens and 2 aces had been played in the first round of hands, and no low cards came out of the deck, the running count would be −18.

But, consider what the balance would look like if this situation occurred while playing in a 6-deck shoe game. To start with, six full decks contain 96 tens and 24 aces. The high card points balanced against the low card points, look like this:

Now, if we remove 8 tens and 2 aces, our balance looks like this:

$$\frac{198}{216} = .92 = 92\%$$

The balance is only slightly tipped because there were so many more points to start with. Although the same cards have been removed as in our single-deck example, we still have 92% as many high card points as low card points in the shoe. What this means to the card counter is that although his running count may be −18 in both situations, his advantage, and his playing strategy, would differ. He must consider how many decks are remaining to be played before making his decisions. Running count must be adjusted to reflect a *true count*, based on the *balance* of the high cards to low cards.

You must adjust your running count to true count even at varying points of deck depletion in a single-deck game. A running count of +10 after the first round dealt from a 52-card deck is not the same as a running count of +10 when all but 5 cards have been seen. In the latter example, we would be certain that every one of the unseen cards remaining to be played was a ten, since we know that our running count always totals 0 when we count through the whole deck.

True Count by Division

All of the Zen strategy indices are based on true count. Insurance, for instance, is recommended if your true count is +5 or more. If you always took insurance at a *running count* of +5 or more, you would lose more money on this bet than you would win, in four and six-deck games. In single-deck games, on the other hand, if you always insured at a *running* count of +5, you would often fail to take insurance when you should.

There are numerous methods of adjusting running count to true count. The most common method is to divide the running count by the number of remaining decks. The chief difficulty of this method is that it often involves dividing by fractions. For instance, most people would find it awkward to quickly divide a running count of +17 by 1½ remaining decks. The true count here is +11. In a single-deck game, you might have to quickly divide −8 by ¾. This true count would be −11.

True Count by Multiplication

An easier method, which is used by some players who have difficulty with division—and, remember, these calculations must be made in the midst of casino play, with no hesitation—is to *multiply* the index number of the decision in question by the number of remaining decks, then compare this number to the running count. For instance, let's say you are trying to decide whether or not to take insurance in a 6-deck game with a running count of +17. Two decks have been played, so 4 remain. Since your insurance index number is +5, you multiply +5 x 4 (remaining decks) = +20. You would not take insurance here because your running count of +17 is not high enough.

Again, the major difficulty of this method arises when fractions are involved. Although most people may find multiplication by fractions easier than division by fractions, the average person finds neither form of arithmetic easy. Most professional players I know don't actually perform this arithmetic at the tables. If you ask a pro, "What's 11 times 1½?" he'll often respond, "17", with no hesitation. He is not necessarily that fast at arithmetic, as you might think. He has simply memorized fractional multiplication (or division) tables in order to eliminate the arithmetic. In 3rd grade, you probably learned multiplication tables for whole numbers from 2 through 12. It's no more difficult to learn tables for fractions, and if you choose to employ one of the above mentioned methods of true count adjustment, it may be necessary. Most people are not comfortable doing arithmetic while playing blackjack in a casino.

True Count Without Fractions

My favorite method of true count adjustment, however, eliminates the need for using fractions in your arithmetic, or learning fractional multiplication tables. This method was taught to me by a player and correspondent who had developed it for his own use. To use this method of true count adjustment, you simply divide your running count (which is always a whole number) by the index number of the decision you are considering (also always a whole number). For example, your running count is +10, and you want to know whether or not you should take insurance. Your insurance index number is +5. Divide 10 by 5, and your answer is 2. This means you should take insurance if there are 2 *or fewer* remaining decks. If more than two decks remain, insurance is a bad bet with a running count of +10. Although, when you use this method, there will never be fractions involved in your division, there will often be fractions in your answers. For instance, if your running count is +17, and you are making your insurance decision, you would have to divide 17 by 5. In this case, insurance is a good bet if $3\,^2/_5$ *or fewer* decks remain. You could round this off to 3 decks or less. If you find it easier to divide 17 by 5, than to either multiply or divide by 1½ or ¾, then you would probably find this method to be your preferred method of true count adjustment. One of the nicest features about this method of adjustment is the ease with which you can make decisions in single-deck games. For example, you want to know if you should insure with a running count of +2. Two divided by 5 quickly gives you the fraction 2/5. You should insure only if 2/5 *or less* of the deck remains.

When you use method 3, you disregard the minus (−) sign, if your running count and index number are both negative. For instance, let's say you're dealt a hand totaling 13 vs. a dealer 3. Your running count is −6. Your Zen Count standing index number for this decision is −4. You don't have to pay any attention to these minus signs, since a negative divided by a negative is always positive. Simply divide 6 by 4 = 1½. Thus, if 1½ *or fewer* decks remain, you would hit. Otherwise, follow basic strategy and stand.

If your running count is negative, and your index number is positive, *or vice versa*, don't bother to make any true count adjustment using any method. Simply follow basic strategy. You'll find that for most strategy decisions you will not have to recall any index number, or adjust your running count for true count. Most often, you'll play basic strategy.

Estimating the Remaining Decks

One art you will have to perfect, regardless of your method of true count adjustment, is estimating the number of remaining decks. You cannot do this without practice.

Buy yourself a few dozen decks of standard playing cards. Use casino-quality cards, preferably used cards obtained from a casino, so that the thickness of the decks is the same as you will encounter in casino play. Many casinos sell their used decks for 25¢ to 75¢ in their gift shops. Make up stacks of cards containing 6 decks, 5½ decks, 5, 4½, 4, 3½, 3, 2½, 2, 1½ and 1. Familiarize yourself with exactly what each sized stack looks like. When you practice true count adjustments, regardless of the method you choose, look at the various sized stacks as you make your adjustments.

In a casino, you won't be looking at such exactly sized stacks of discards very often, but your eyes will estimate to the nearest sized stack with which you have familiarized yourself, so that you can make your adjustments effortlessly.

Never waste a moment in this estimation process. If it appears 1¼ decks are remaining, don't teeter between calling it 1 or 1½. Call it 1½. Always round *up*. This way you'll play more conservatively. Call it 1 only when it's *definitely* below 1¼.

Also, when you eyeball one of your practice stacks, remember that you are looking at the *discards*. Therefore, if you are assuming you are in a 6-deck game, and you look at a stack of 4 decks, you will be making your true count adjustment based on 2 decks—the *remaining* decks. Be sure you practice this way.

I know of one player who practiced eyeballing various sized stacks of cards, then adjusting his running count to true count, until he had it down to perfection. He got to Las Vegas and realized he'd learned the whole thing backwards. He was making his true count adjustments as if the discards were the remaining cards, instead of the other way around.

A mistake like this would be costly. You'd be better off playing basic strategy and not counting cards at all.

True count adjustment is one of the most difficult aspects of card counting to master. Most counters are ill-trained in this area. Almost all successful blackjack pros are experts at adjusting to true count.

If you ever try to join a professional blackjack team, don't be surprised if you're tested rigorously on true count adjustments. The team captain will likely show you various-sized stacks of discards and give you hypothetical strategy decisions. He will expect you to respond with the proper plays immediately, based on your system. After each response, you'll have to explain in detail the methodology you followed in making your decision.

I'm always surprised by sloppy, slow, and ill-trained players, who believe they would be winning fortunes if they just had the big bankroll behind them. When they do get money behind them—their own, or other people's—they lose it in no time at all. Then they complain about cheating dealers, poor conditions, negative fluctuations, etc. These players, *and the majority of card counters fall into this group*, are the meat and potatoes of the casino industry.

♣♦♠♥

BETTING STRATEGIES

There is one concept behind all betting strategies for card counters: bet more when you have the edge, less when the house has the edge.

A number of factors complicate this dictum. First, you must know *how much* more to bet when you have the edge. Second, you must raise your bet so that you do not attract attention to yourself. Third, your bankroll must be sufficient to withstand the fluctuations.

Single-Deck Betting Strategies

First, estimate the size of your high bet, according to the size of your bankroll. In single-deck games, your high bet should be your bankroll divided by 100. Given a $1,000 bankroll, your high bet should be $10. You must constantly reassess the size of your bankroll as you play, and alter the size of your bets accordingly. (See Chapter Four.) This need not be a difficult accounting procedure. You know the size of your bankroll prior to beginning play. Now keep track of how much of your money you pull out of your pockets. Always buy chips in small amounts. If you're playing with nickels ($5 chips), don't buy in for more than $100, and $20 is enough if you're using a 1-to-2 spread. If you're playing with quarters ($25 chips), you need not buy in for more than $500, and $200 may be sufficient as an initial buy-in, if you're using a small spread. If you need more chips, you can always pull more money out of your pocket. Pit bosses are sometimes wary of players who buy in for stacks and stacks of chips. Casino floormen like to see players digging into their pockets for more money, since this indicates the player has been losing. By keeping track of how much money you pull from your pocket, you can reassess your bankroll by counting up your chips every hour or so. When there is a significant change in your bankroll, divide by 100 to determine the size of your high bet. Most of the time, you will approximate this bet size. For instance, with a $3,150 bankroll, your optimal high bet would be:

$$\$3,150 \div 100 = \$31.50$$

Your high bet would be $30. Remember that you will experience wild swings of positive and negative fluctuations. On occasion, you may have to reassess after only 10 minutes of play. If you fail to reassess your bankroll often enough, it could be devastating to you in a few hours. You must cut back when you lose and you must do it quickly. Try to reassess after winning or losing ten high bets. With a high bet of $25, you should stop and reassess after winning or losing about $250. Again, if you keep track of how much cash you've pulled out of your pocket, this is automatic.

Once you find your optimal high bet you must determine your low bet. This is determined by the table conditions.

The most commonly available single-deck games are:
* Vegas Strip
* Vegas Downtown (Hits Soft 17)
* Reno (Hits Soft 17; Double 10, 11 only)
* Reno (Same, but no Insurance)

The betting spread you need to beat each game depends on what percentage of the cards you have been able to see and count, *and* make a final bet based on that count. You should be able to get an edge of about 1% by using the recommendations in this table:

Single-Deck Spread Table

Game	40%	50%	60%	70%
Vegas Strip	1-4	1-3	1-2	1-2
Vegas Downtown	D.P.	1-3	1-2	1-2
Reno	D.P.	D.P.	1-3	1-2
Reno (N.I.)	D.P.	D.P.	1-4	1-3

(D.P. = Don't Play)

64

Now you can determine your betting strategy for any single-deck game. If a casino offers some rule variation which is not in this table, such as surrender, or double-after-splits, use the betting strategy for the most similar game in this table. (If you do not recall the rules of the games listed here, see Chapter Six.)

If you've determined your optimal high bet to be $30, and you're playing in single-deck downtown Vegas games, then you can see from the table that you *must* be able to count at least 50% of the cards prior to making your final bet before the shuffle. If the dealer shuffles before this depth of the deal occurs, then you should not play. If the shuffle is sufficiently deep to make this game profitable, you should use a 1-to-3 spread ($10 to $30). If you can count more than 60% of the cards prior to your final bet, then you can beat this game with only a 1-to-2 spread ($15 to $30).

If you use the Red Seven Count, you raise your bet at the pivot. If you use the Zen Count, raise your bet when the edge has turned to your favor by at least ½% (see Chapter Seven). If you are using a 1-to-2 spread, always raise and lower your bets precisely, according to your advantage. If you are using a larger spread, do not *jump* your bets, but *graduate* them; i.e., never follow a 1-unit bet with a 3-unit bet. You must graduate from 1 to 2 to 3 units. When using a 1-to-4 spread, you may graduate from 1 to 2 to 4, but only graduate to 4 units *after a 2-unit win.* For example, if your count is high, and you have just lost a 2-unit bet, you should not graduate to a 4-unit bet, but bet 2 units again. This will keep you looking less like a card counter, and more like a typical gambler, parlaying when you win. If you are a good actor, you may get away with jumping bets, and even larger spreads than recommended here. You might do this by acting like a gambler who is upping his bets to chase his losses. After many hours in casinos, you will learn to recognize this compulsize type of behavior, and you may be able to put on a convincing act yourself. Unless you're a good actor, you should stick with the lowest recommended betting spreads. A wider spread will increase your win rate, but don't take unnecessary chances.

If you use the Zen Count (but *not* the Red Seven Count), you can beat the single-deck Vegas games sufficiently with a flat bet if 80% or more of the cards can be counted between shuffles. I recommend this for high stakes players who are likely to get heat. If your starting bankroll is under $5,000, you would also be wise to employ "one-deck Wonging", a betting strategy described in Chapter Ten.

Two-Deck Games

Two-deck games are not common, so remember these guidelines. With Northern Nevada (Reno) rules, play in one-deck games only, which are most commonly available. In Las Vegas, play in 2-deck games only if at least 75% (1½ decks) are dealt out between shuffles. You must use at least a 1-to-4 spread to get a 1% edge in these games. Calculate your high bet for 2-deck games as your bankroll divided by 120, instead of 100, as for single-deck games.

Four-or-More-Deck Games

For games with 4 decks, estimate your high bet as your bankroll divided by 150. For six-deck games, your high bet is your bankroll divided by 175. With eight decks, divide your bankroll by 200 to estimate your high bet.

When you are playing vs. four or more decks, you must "table-hop". This technique is often called "Wonging" by card counters, after blackjack pro Stanford Wong, who popularized this playing style. Wonging is refusing to play vs. negative situations. When your count indicates that the house has any significant edge, you leave the table to find a better game. On the first couple of rounds after a shuffle, you may tolerate a *low* negative *running* count, −2 to –3. After the third round, stay only if the count is plus. If you are in a large casino, and there are many open table opportunities, do not play vs. *any* negative running count.

In Nevada casinos, your best approach to table-hopping is to keep your eyes open as you walk through the blackjack pits. When you spot a crowded table covered with low (plus) cards, get as accurate of a count as you can, and get a bet (or bets) onto any open betting spaces. If you are using the Red Seven Count, you are seeking tables with running counts at (or close to) your pivot. The Red Seven Count is particularly powerful for this playing style. Its betting efficiency is high, and all of its variations from basic strategy are plus-count variations.

If you are using the Zen Count, you are seeking tables where your true count indicates that you have the edge. This will depend on the number of decks, rules, etc. (Chapters Six, Seven, and Eight). If table-hopping is your only style of play, you need not learn the Zen Count strategy indices below −1, since you would not be encountering these decisions. You may also want to learn a few more of the Zen plus-count indices, from the Appendix, if you have a good memory. The Stand decisions are the most important.

When table-hopping, you will sometimes walk for long periods without placing a bet. You will sometimes play only one hand before the count goes down again. For this reason it's best to cover two (or more) betting spots when you find an advantageous betting situation.

Your table-hopping must appear natural or you will be recognized as a counter. You cannot stand behind a table and count for round after round, jumping in only when the count goes up. This is obvious. You must appear casual. Table-hopping is probably easiest to pull off when you are with a companion of the opposite sex. While searching for good tables, you can act like you're more interested in each other, wandering around like lovers at a carnival.

In Atlantic City, casinos may restrict bets to the table minimum of any player who enters a game after the shuffle. This rule is specifically designed to foil Wongers. In casinos where this rule is enforced, the only way to table-hop is to enter games right after the shuffle, stay if the count goes up, and leave if it goes down, in search of another newly shuffled shoe. You may jump your bets in Atlantic City from table minimum to table maximum, without fear of being barred, but the dealer may shuffle-up on you at any time. How strictly the Atlantic City casinos will enforce these options remains to be seen. But, no card counting strategy can significantly beat a six- or eight-deck game, if less than 65% of the cards are dealt out, unless you are allowed to table-hop.

When table-hopping, you may either use a betting spread, or flat bet. Flat-betting will work only if you wait until you have a decided edge until entering a game. Otherwise, you must spread your bets, at least 1-to-4 units, and often higher. Remember to only raise your bet after a win, by parlaying. If you attempt raising after a loss, you must appear to be chasing your losses, as a compulsive gambler might. To pull this off you may have to make comments to the dealer, other players, etc., about "feeling a winning streak coming up," "ending a losing streak", etc. Many of the most successful card counters are those who can convince the casinos that they are die-hard gamblers. Some of these players use phenomenal betting spreads, sometimes 1-to-100 units, by being good actors.

Any multi-deck game in which 50% or more of the cards are being cut off will offer very slim pickings to the card counter, regardless of betting strategy.

If you use the Zen Count, remember when adjusting to true count that this adjustment is based on *unseen* cards. If you enter a 4-deck game in progress after counting only one round, you must keep aware of the fact that you have seen and counted very few cards. There may be two decks already in the discard pile. Do not make your true count adjustments according to the discards, other than for those you have seen and counted (Chapter Eight).

The betting spread you will need to beat any game depends on how frequently you play in negative situations. This depends on the number of decks shuffled together, the depth of the deal, and the count at which you enter and/or quit the game. If you play through all positive counts, but quit at any negative count, you would need to use the following spreads to obtain a significant edge (about 1%), according to shuffle-point and number of decks:

Multi-Deck Spread Table

	50%	60%	70%	80%
4 Decks	D.P.	1-16	1-8	1-4
6 Decks	D.P.	D.P.	1-16	1-8
8 Decks	D.P.	D.P.	D.P.	1-16
9+ Decks	D.P.	D.P.	D.P.	D.P.

(D.P. = Don't Play)

Multi-deck games restrict profitable playing conditions for players with limited bankrolls. For example, suppose you find a 6-deck game with a 70% shuffle-point. The table minimum bet is $2. According to the betting spread chart, you should use a 1-to-16 spread to get a good edge in this game, even if you leave the table at any negative count. This means you must spread your bets at least from $2 to $32. Since, for 6-deck games, your high bet is optimally your bankroll divided by 175, then in order to make this high bet of $32, you would have to have at least 175 x $32 = $5,600. The Multi-Deck Spread Table is designed to get you an advantage of about 1%. You may find that the only games available, or your limited bankroll, make this impossible.

The only way to compensate for this, if you do not have a sufficient bankroll, is to play less frequently under unfavorable circumstances. Instead of playing through all positive counts, and quitting only when the count turns negative, you would have to play *only* when you had the decided edge, i.e., at or above your pivot with the Red Seven Count, or when your true count indicated you had the edge with the Zen Count. In this way, you could use a smaller spread, and a smaller, affordable high bet, and still get an edge over the house. The difficulty is that you may not find enough betting situations to be worth the time spent looking.

For ease of reference, this chart indicates your high bet as a proportion of your bankroll for any number of decks.

HIGH BETS PER BANKROLL

# Decks	Bankroll Divided By
1	100
2	120
4	150
6	175
8	200

Playing Simultaneous Hands

When you are table-hopping, you will often place bets on more than one spot at a time. This will increase the fluctuation of your bankroll. To decrease the fluctuation to an affordable level, you should cut back on the size of your high bet. If you play 2 hands, both hands together should equal about 1½ times your standard high bet. If you play 3 *or more* hands, the total amount of money you place on the table should not be more than double your standard high bet.

Example: According to the game you are playing, and the size of your bankroll, you estimate your high bet to be $40 when you are playing a single spot. An opportunity occurs for you to bet on two spots. Your bets should not total more than *1½ times* your $40 high bet, so:

$$1½ \times \$40 = \$60$$

You would place two bets of *$30 each*.

Later, an opportunity occurs for you to play three simultaneous hands. Your three bets should not total more than *double* your $40 high bet.

$$2 \times \$40 = \$80$$

You may place 3 bets of $25 each; or, if convenient, two $25 bets and one $30 bet. If an opportunity should arise for you to place 4 simultaneous bets, you would still be limited to placing a total amount on the table of $80, or four $20 bets. Unless you have a very large bankroll, it's not usually practical to play more than 3 simultaneous hands.

"Kelly betting" is attempting to bet a proportion of your bankroll equal to your advantage over the house. This means that with a 1% edge you would bet 1% of your bankroll. Theoretically, this is the fastest way to increase the size of your bankroll. Practically, it's impossible to follow such a betting scheme strictly since it's impossible to know your precise advantage in the game of blackjack. Table-hoppers, however, may use a conservative Kelly-type betting system to their advantage. I would advise it for Zen Count players only.

In Chapter Seven, it was stated that each true point, using the Zen Count, raises your edge by about ¼%. This is a conservative estimate, more or less accurate at the beginning of a newly shuffled shoe. When you are down to the last deck of the shoe, each true point is worth more, and towards the end of this last deck, each true point is worth close to ½%. This is due to the "strategy gain" from accurately employing the Zen Count indices. Because "true" count is imprecise, any attempt to follow a strict Kelly betting system is futile. I suggest the following simplified approach:

1. Divide your total Bankroll by 600, to determine the size of one *Kelly unit*. With a $3,000 bankroll:

$$\text{Kelly Unit} = \$3,000 \div 600 = \$5$$

2. Determine the point at which the Zen Count indicates you have a ¼% edge, depending on rules, decks, etc., assuming each Zen true point is worth ¼%. In the 4-deck Vegas Strip game, for instance, this occurs at a true count of +3.

3. Bet one Kelly unit when you have a ¼% edge, and add one Kelly unit for each true count over and above this point. Thus, with a true count of +4, in the 4-deck Strip game, you would bet 2 Kelly units. With a true count of +12, you would bet **10 Kelly units.**

Using the Zen Count in a 4-deck game with Vegas Strip rules, you will occasionally see true counts as high as +20. This would call for a bet of **18 Kelly units.** With a $3,000 bankroll, and a $5 Kelly unit, this bet would be $80.

A Kelly bettor will place more money on the table than a player who bets according to a set "high bet", as recommended earlier in this chapter. The Kelly bettor will increase the size of his bankroll faster, *if he reassesses his bankroll size often, and adjusts his Kelly unit accordingly.* Your fluctuation using a Kelly betting system will be much greater than your fluctuation using the standard high-bet betting system. You should not use a Kelly betting system if you have difficulty monitoring your bankroll, especially during losing streaks.

Kelly bettors should follow the same guidelines for playing simultaneous hands as other bettors. If you play two simultaneous hands, both bets together should equal only 1½ times your optimal Kelly bet. With 3 or more simultaneous hands, you should not place a total amount of money on the table more than double your optimal Kelly bet.

If you play well, in favorable games, according to the guidelines of this chapter, and if you always reassess your bankroll after winning or losing 10 high bets, you will never lose all your money. You may lose enough of your money due to normal fluctuation, that you can no longer afford to play according to the guidelines of this chapter. However, you have about a 95% chance of doubling your bankroll before this occurs. If you want to cut this risk back to only a 1% chance of losing this much of your bankroll, then double the recommended numbers by which you divide your bankroll to obtain your high bet. For playing in 4-deck games, for instance, find your optimal high bet by dividing your bankroll by 300, instead of 150 or find your optimal Kelly unit by dividing by 1,200, instead of 600. Your could almost insure yourself of staying in the game *forever*—assuming you're an expert player—by determining your *high bet* by dividing your bankroll by 1,000. It would be rare for a good player, playing in beatable games, with a $10,000 bankroll, to lose it all, due to normal fluctuation, if he was making high bets of $10. Unfortunately, if you have sufficient funds to play blackjack risk-free, the return on your investment would be too low for the game to be worth your time as a profit-making venture. If you just enjoy playing the game for fun, you may be happy making $2 bets regardless of the size of your bankroll. If your bankroll is dear to you, and you cannot accept the fact that there is risk involved in this game, you should not play. If you like money risks, this game is thrilling. It's like putting your money on a roller coaster. It's not something you do with your rent money.

♣♦♠♥

10
THE UNENCOUNTERED COUNTER

A master of any martial art does not conquer his opponent; rather he allows his opponent to conquer himself. The opponent's strengths are in essence turned against the opponent's weaknesses. The opponent loses the battle because he is fighting himself. The master wins not because he is physically stronger, but because he is mentally a step ahead of his opponent. The master is an invisible catalyst. The opponent never sees his downfall coming. His own strength and momentum are hurling him to the ground while he is busy watching out for the master's attack.

Playing blackjack for profit is a similar situation. Your opponent, the casino, has vast strength in the form of an incredibly large bankroll. Furthermore, the house sets all the rules of the "fight" and may eliminate any opponent it considers a worthy challenge. This is a tough set-up. Not only do you have to play very well in order to win, but, if you *look like* you play very well, you may not be allowed to play at all.

The major weakness of the casinos is that their advantage over the player is *volatile*. Sometimes they have a large edge, but other times they are at a disadvantage to the knowledgeable player.

In the same way that a martial arts master does not depend on his muscles to win a fight, a master of blackjack does not depend on some incredibly difficult, higher level, multi-parameter counting system to win money at the tables. Rather, he allows the volatility of the game to put money into his pockets at its own rate. He remains invisible as a counter because he is not exploiting his own strengths as much as he is exploiting the casino's weaknesses.

Single-deck games are volatile. The change in advantage is fast and great. Multi-deck games are less volatile. The change in the edge is slow. The master counter employs a different strategy for each game, designed to eliminate his encounters with the casino *as a counter* while at the same time maximizing his win rate. These are some of his strategies:

Depth-Charging: A Single-Deck Strategy

Casinos identify counters by watching for bet variation. If you don't bet like a counter you will not usually be considered a counter, regardless of how accurately you might be playing your cards. It is very easy for a "counter catcher" to count down a deck from behind or above you, using any card counting system, while monitoring your bet size. Regardless of what counting system you are using, your bet sizing will give you away. A level-one Red Seven Count player would raise and lower bets similarly to a level-two Zen Count player. A counter using any other system would have no difficulty in detecting the conspicuous betting patterns of either player.

Most camouflage techniques employed by counters are methods of disguising bet variation. Such techniques inevitably hurt your potential win rate, but without camouflage you will be frequently shuffled up on and probably barred if you play for high stakes.

"Depth-charging" is a single-deck strategy which allows you to play a winning game without using a betting spread based on your count. This strategy is for Zen Count players *only*. The Red Seven Count does *not* provide enough variations from basic strategy to make depth-charging profitable. Red Seven Count players may want to skim this section for background information, but otherwise, should skip ahead to the next section of this chapter: "One-Deck Wonging".

According to Peter Griffin's *Theory of Blackjack* (page 28), the potential gain from computer-perfect play depends on the number of cards which have been seen. As more cards are seen, the greater the gain. I've simplified Griffin's charts here to show how much the player can gain from the combined "perfect" playing strategy variations and insurance decisions. The player is flat-betting in a single-deck Vegas Strip game:

GAIN TABLE	
% Cards Seen	% Gain
13%	.16%
23%	.33%
33%	.53%
42%	.80%
52%	1.18%
62%	1.68%
71%	2.46%
81%	3.80%

If you always "back-counted" this single-deck game (i.e., counting while watching others play), only playing a hand after you'd seen 81% of the cards (42 cards), and if you made computer-perfect playing decisions, you could win at the rate of 3.8%, *even if you always flat bet, and played this one hand regardless of whether the count had been positive or negative.*

Unfortunately, you cannot play this way. Back counting a single-deck game like this would get you booted out of most casinos quickly. Put aside for the moment the fact that this is not a practical strategy, and consider *why* this strategy would be so profitable. Your edge off the top of the deck is about even. As you go deeper into the deck, the count fluctuates, but you are just as likely to see a count of −10 as +10 if you are using a balanced count system. So why would perfect play, regardless of count, be worth so much?

Let's consider one playing variation only: insurance. What is insurance worth off the top of the deck? Nothing. After seeing only your two cards and the dealer's ace, it would never be the correct play. Is insurance worthless half way through the deck? Absolutely not. It's true that a count of −10 will occur just as frequently as a count of +10, but you don't lose a penny on insurance when the count is −10 *because your count tells you not to take it.* When the count is +10, you have a decided edge on this bet. The insurance edge is volatile, and most of the time, the house has the edge. However, the volatility of the edge always works in favor of the knowledgeable player who has the option of altering strategy. The house is not allowed to take insurance if you are dealt an ace for your first card. Likewise, the house is not allowed to stand on 16 if the count is high, etc.

Let's go back to the gain table:

If you didn't back-count, but simply played head-to-head with the dealer, always flat-betting, but again, with computer-perfect decisions, your potential win rate can be approximated by averaging the gains at each level. You may now estimate your potential flat-bet win rate at various shuffle points, employing the Zen Count, for this single-deck game. To understand depth-charging, and to devise depth-charging strategies, you must understand how to use the gain table. So let's estimate the win rate for a Zen Count player who is playing head-to-head in this game with a shuffle-point of slightly better than 50%. In single-deck Vegas Strip games, this is pretty close to what you might expect to find.

First, we find the "average" gain. To do this, we add together the gains at all deck levels up to 52%:

$$
\begin{array}{r}
.16 \\
.33 \\
.53 \\
.80 \\
\underline{1.18} \\
3.00\%
\end{array}
$$

Second, we divide this total gain by the number of hands we have played:

$$5 \overline{)3.00} \quad .60\%$$

And third, we multiply this "computer perfect" total gain by the Zen system's playing efficiency. For the Zen Count, this is *.63*:

$$.60\% \times .63 = .378\%$$

Thus, we estimate a Zen Count player's potential flat-bet gain to be slightly less than .4% in this game.

Definition: "Depth-charging" is using the depth of the deal as the primary method of gaining a long-run advantage, rather than relying on a betting spread based on card counting information. Since casinos often recognize the traditional betting strategies of card counters, the depth-charger employs a betting strategy which is not based on his count. He *always* bets more deep in the deck, even when his count is negative. His playing strategy is so much more effective deep in the deck, that he obtains a significant edge over the house.

Example: Suppose this Zen Count player, rather than flat betting, added a chip with each successive round until the shuffle. Let's keep the same shuffle point of slightly better than 50%. The math used to estimate win rate now looks like this:

% Gain		# Chips		Total Gain
.16	X	1	=	.16
.33	X	2	=	.66
.53	X	3	=	1.59
.80	X	4	=	3.20
1.18	X	5	=	5.90
Sums :		15	,	11.51%

Now, we must divide the total gain by the total chips bet:

$$11.51\% \div 15 = .767\%$$

Now multiply this "computer perfect" gain by the Zen Count's playing efficiency:

$$.767\% \times .63 = .483\%$$

Thus, this betting strategy has raised the potential win rate from .38% to .48%, without using the count information for betting purposes. A player employing such a strategy would probably not be viewed as a counter, because of his unwavering progression-type betting system. This example is not an approach I would recommend, but is provided to illustrate the theory behind depth-charging strategies.

Now what about a more radical approach? Again, this is for the purpose of explanation. It is not a recommended, or even a highly effective, depth-charging strategy. Let's say you start with one chip, then double your bet after every hand. Using $5 chips, you would bet $5, $10, $20, $40, then $80. In units, this would be 1, 2, 4, 8, 16:

% Gain		# Chips		Total Gain
.16	X	1	=	.16
.33	X	2	=	.66
.53	X	4	=	2.12
.80	X	8	=	6.40
1.18	X	16	=	18.88
Sums :		31	,	28.22%

Divide total gain by total chips bet:

$$28.22\% \div 31 = .910\%$$

Multiply the "perfect" gain by the Zen Count's playing efficiency:

$$.91\% \times .63 = .573\%$$

Thus, we have raised our flat-bet gain from .38% to .57% without using a betting strategy based on card counting information. Such a strategy may actually *encourage* a dealer to deal deeper. If he *knows* you are using a progression system, and the deeper he deals, the bigger your bet, he may be tempted to go one more round just to see you add another chip, or double up again. To your advantage, the deeper the deal, the more substantial is your potential gain from depth-charging. For instance, your average flat-bet gain, at a shuffle-point of 71% (rather than 52% as above), using the Zen Count, is about .64%. If you use the add-one-chip strategy, your potential win rate comes to .87%. With the double-up strategy, as above, you would raise this potential gain to 1.19%, almost double your expected flat-bet gain. The above examples are crude illustrations of depth-charging. Far more effective strategies can be devised.

The method of predicting gain used thus far is approximate, and somewhat exaggerated. We can get better accuracy, and make the calculations simpler, by drawing up a set of gain tables more pertinent to depth-charging strategies. First of all, Griffin's tables, upon which the above examples are based, list the gains in five-card increments, working from 47 cards unseen down. Actually, an average round of play, head-on, will use about 5.4 cards, and your first round advantage will simply be your basic strategy advantage. Your second-round decision will thus be made after approximately 8.4 cards have been seen, 5.4 cards from the first round, then your two cards and the dealer's up-card on the second round. Successive head-on rounds should be estimated as being played in 5.4 card increments; round 3: 13.8 cards; round 4: 19.2 cards; etc.

We can also simplify the math by assuming a count system with a playing efficiency of about 60%, and listing all gains in our tables based on this assumption. These are the gain tables for head-on single-deck games on the Vegas Strip, in Downtown Vegas, and Northern Nevada. The tables take into account the house edge and the rule variations. All gains are conservative estimates, rounded to .05% to make estimations easier.

GAIN TABLES:

SINGLE-DECK, HEAD-ON, 60% EFFICIENCY

Vegas Strip

% Dealt	Round	Gain
-	1	0.00
16	2	+0.10
27	3	+0.30
37	4	+0.45
47	5	+0.70
58	6	+1.00
68	7	+1.40
78	8	+1.90

Vegas Downtown

-	1	-0.20
16	2	-0.10
27	3	+0.10
37	4	+0.25
47	5	+0.50
58	6	+0.80
68	7	+1.15
78	8	+1.70

Northern Nevada

-	1	-0.50
16	2	-0.35
27	3	-0.20
37	4	0.00
47	5	+0.20
58	6	+0.50
68	7	+0.90
78	8	+1.40

Now, what would be your flat-bet win rate in each game, assuming 7 rounds of play (shuffle point of about 68%)? By adding the gains through 7 rounds for each game, then dividing by 7, we get:

Vegas Strip:	+ .56%
Vegas Downtown:	+ .36%
Northern Nevada:	+ .08%

Using the add-one-chip-per-round method:

Vegas Strip:	+ .79%
Vegas Downtown:	+ .58%
Northern Nevada:	+ .30%

Using the double-up method:

Vegas Strip:	+1.09%
Vegas Downtown:	+ .86%
Northern Nevada:	+ .63%

Note that if using the double-up method, by the seventh round you would be betting 64 units. Thus, if your unit was $2, your seventh-round bet would be $128. With a $5 unit, your seventh-round bet would be $320. For this reason, I view this head-on double-up betting strategy as more theoretical than practical. You would, in all likelihood, be viewed by the casino as more of a lunatic than a card counter if you could afford to bet in this fashion, but again, these strategies are offered more to illustrate the mechanics of depth-charging than to encourage you to employ these betting styles. If you do attempt to use a double-up betting strategy, don't overbet your bankroll. If the dealer starts to deal deeper just to get your big money on the table, don't be tempted to double your bet when you can't afford it. An eighth-round double-up bet on a $2 unit would be $256. With a $5 unit, the eighth-round bet would be $640. If your bankroll isn't large enough to justify such bets, don't make them. Determine your maximum bet and simply let it ride once you've hit the top, until the shuffle. Another note of caution: if the dealer shuffles up when the count is high, but deals deeply when the count is low, depth-charging will *not* work. Most dealers pay no attention to the count unless they suspect a counter. Still, depth-charging can be used to greater advantage, more practically, and with a far less radical betting approach at crowded tables. I don't personally view depth-charging as an advisable strategy for head-to-head play.

Since developing this strategy (some six months prior to the publication of this book), a number of professional players have devised effective head-on methods of depth-charging with which you may want to experiment. All of these methods involve playing multiple simultaneous hands, betting more on subsequent rounds, and betting larger on the third base side of the table (which hands will be played after seeing more cards). Camouflage is sometimes provided by haphazardly sizing bets on the first round (and/or the first base side of the table). Some of the spots on the first base side may also be played using useless progression systems, with sizeably smaller bets than those being placed on the third base side, etc. But depth-charging is often more advantageous with more people at the table. That is, if you know how to do it...

For example: you sit on the left side of two players. Because the three of you are in adjacent seats, you have no trouble seeing both players' down cards as they look at them. And because they are sitting to your right, both of them will play their hands first. Sometimes they will hit and sometimes not, but *on the average*, each player will take one hit card each prior to your playing your hand. Thus, on the average, your *first hand* will be played after having seen: the dealer's up-card, both players' down cards, one hit card for each player, and your own two down cards, for a total of 9 cards (17% of the deck). Your second round will be played after seeing, on the average, one hit card for yourself and 1.4 cards for the dealer (to complete the first round), then another dealer up-card, two more cards for each player, including yourself, and one more hit card for each player to your right—for a total of 11.4 cards. Add this to the 9 cards you saw prior to playing your second hand, and your second hand would be played on the average after seeing 20.4 cards (or 39% of the deck). The third-round hand would average another 11.4 cards seen before you play, for 31.8 cards, or 61% of the deck. If there is a fourth round, you will have seen 43.2 cards, or 83% of the deck. (In Northern Nevada, there will almost always be a fourth round when three players are at the table in single-deck games. In Las Vegas, it will depend on the casino and the dealer.)

Let's draw up some gain tables for this game.

	Vegas Strip		Northern Nevada	
% Dealt	Round	Gain	Round	Gain
17%	1	+0.15%	1	-0.35%
39%	2	+0.50%	2	0.00%
61%	3	+1.10%	3	+0.55%
83%	4	+2.25%	4	+1.80%

Using the same method to calculate the potential win rates for the betting approaches analyzed previously, we find:

With 3 Rounds

	Vegas	Northern Nevada
Flat-Bet:	.58%	+ .07%
Add-A-Chip:	.74%	+ .22%
Double-Up:	.79%	+ .26%

With 4 Rounds

	Vegas	Northern Nevada
Flat-Bet:	1.00%	+ .50%
Add-A-Chip:	1.35%	+ .85%
Double-Up:	1.57%	+1.08%

Not only are the potential win rates higher here than for head-on play, but the actual bet-sizing is more realistic. Even with 4 rounds, a double-up bet only goes to eight chips. And you would still appear to be more of a gambler than a card counter.

A husband/wife team wrote to me that they used this method of play successfully in a unique partnership approach. The wife sat to the right of the husband and played 3 spots with low bets. On every hand, she consulted her husband on how to play. In fact, she did not know basic strategy. The husband sometimes gave her correct advice, sometimes less than correct—which made him appear more like a show-off than a knowledgeable player. He, meanwhile, played either one or two spots on the third base side of the table, at substantially higher stakes than his wife. He always played his own hands according to the correct count strategy.

Of course the ultimate in depth-charging strategy would be to sit in the third base (far left) position, *at a full table,* with a full view of all players' down cards. Practically, however, it is not possible to see all players' down cards prior to playing your hand. On rare occasions you might get this much information, but not with consistency. Various players are more or less guarded about flashing their cards, and your angle, from third base, will hide the cards of the players on the first base (far right) side of the table.

So for practical purposes, you would be better off to take a central position at a full table, where you could conceivably catch the down cards of the two players to your right, and the two to your left. Again, players who are guarded about flashing their cards to other players may stymie your efforts to read even these four players' cards. If this is the case, you would be best off to find a new table. Many players are not so guarded, and you will find that from the center seat you may often see even the first and/or third base players' cards. I've found it necessary, at times, to sit down at half-a-dozen tables before finding one where enough players expose their down cards. You must be careful not to act overly interested in other players' hands, since this may look suspicious. Your primary camouflage, however, which is *not betting according to the count*, should be highly effective in protecting you from suspicion of counting.

Quite often you'll see the cards of the players to your right simply because they bust their hands, double down, split pairs, or show a natural. For this reason, you would be better off with a seat to the left of center at a full table. In practice, you'll find that you cannot choose your seat at full tables with such precision. You have to grab the seat that opens up. Likewise, as you play, players will come and go. Any potential win rate estimated from a gain table is inevitably a rough estimation.

In a single-deck game with a full table, there will usually be two rounds, then a shuffle. Some Las Vegas dealers will deal only a single round in this game but most will deal two. On the average, a single round at a full table uses about 23.4 cards (about 45% of the deck). Although the second round will often deplete the deck, most dealers will deal this round because bets must be placed prior to the deal, when less than half the cards have been seen.

This table shows your single-deck, full table expected win rates, assuming you are in the center seat, and can see on the average four players' down cards other than your own. The betting strategies which can beat this game are either flat betting or using a 1-to-2 spread: simply one chip on the first round, then two on the second.

	Vegas	Northern Nevada
Flat-Bet:	1.1%	+ .6%
1-2 Spread:	1.4%	+ .9%

Look how valuable this 1-to-2 spread is at a full table.

Now, is there some way you could sit at third base and always "see" all players' down cards prior to betting? From your third base position, you would need an "outfielder". An outfielder is a non-player whose job is to observe all players' down cards, then relay the count information to the thirdbaser. This may sound tricky, but it's easier than many "team" approaches to beating blackjack where "spooks" often try to glimpse the dealer's hole card. An outfielder is simply a wife/husband/girlfriend/boyfriend who is standing behind you while you play your cards. From this vantage point, all player down cards may be unsuspectingly read prior to your having to play your hand. Outfielding is not easy. I've tried it in dozens of casinos in Las Vegas, Reno, and Stateline, Nevada. My experience is that you must often try many tables before you find one where the players are loose enough about flashing cards to make depth-charging a viable strategy. Your outfielder passes information to you by a simple touch on your arm or shoulder area, with various areas corresponding to various counts. The right side is positive, the left negative or whatever. There are also various approaches which could involve a counter on the first base side passing signals to a counter on the third base side, and vice versa, via hand positions, body postures, etc. In this way, both players could play with the majority of the full-table depth-charging gain, though neither would be in the optimal third base position. A team of four to seven players could conceivably take over a table, and totally eliminate the need for passing signals simply by flashing all cards to each other. Such a team need not raise casino suspicions if the players are openly friendly with each other, asking advice about how to play their hands, bragging, complaining, etc. Numerous camouflage betting strategies could also be devised for such a team approach so that the end result is that the *table* bets heavier on the second round than the first. Players could take turns making "foolish" bets, etc.

This table shows the approximate potential win rate for the third base player only, with complete down card information, and two rounds in this single-deck game:

	Vegas	Northern Nevada
Flat-Bet:	1.5%	+ 1.0%
1-2 Spread:	1.9%	+ 1.4%

Note the substantial edge you can get in either of these games with just a flat bet. This may seem incredible, but remember that every other hand will be played after counting about 80% of the deck. The volatility of the single-deck game makes this information that valuable.

Can you combine a depth-charging strategy with a traditional card-counting betting strategy? Yes, and this will increase your potential win rate. For instance, in the last example, of a thirdbaser at a full single-deck table, with an outfielder, such a player could increase his 1-to-2 spread edge over the house by about .5% if he only raised his bet when his count indicated that he had an advantage for the second round. In Las Vegas, such a player would thus be playing with a phenomenal 2.4% edge over the house, on this inconspicuous 1-to-2 spread. In Reno, this strategy would provide an expectation of about 1.9%. This combined depth-charging/counting strategy would also significantly cut fluctuation of your bankroll. For a solo player (no outfielder) at full single-deck tables, catching 4 players' hole cards, sitting one seat to the left of center, raising from 1 to 2 chips on the second hand only when the count indicates this to be correct, an edge of close to 2% can be realized on the Vegas Strip, and about 1.5% in Reno. A larger spread would raise your edge even more, but this would be dangerous if you were betting according to the count.

Can you depth-charge in multi-deck games? Yes, but the gains are diminished. Depth-charging is not a practical strategy in multi-deck games. For example, consider a full-table two-deck game, with a depth-charger at third base, with an outfielder. Three rounds will consume close to 70% of the cards, so you're unlikely to get a fourth round. Here's your two-deck gain table.

	Vegas	Northern Nevada
Flat-Bet:	0.0%	-0.4%
Add-A-Chip:	+0.1%	-0.3%
Double-Up:	+0.2%	-0.2%

If you could find a dealer who would consistently give 4 rounds in this game, which would consume about 90% of the cards, a double-up thirdbaser could get about a .9% advantage on the Strip, and about .5% in Reno, but such a game would be hard to find. For 4- and 6-deck games, depth-charging is worthless as a sole strategy. Since these games are often dealt face up, an alert counter uses the available information to his best advantage anyway.

Some of the advantages to depth-charging single-deck games are that crowded tables become beatable; the betting strategy contains a built-in camouflage, and there are numerous opportunities and approaches for partners and teams.

Some of the disadvantages are that crowded tables mean slow play for solo players and signal passing is always dangerous unless you are well practiced.

To devise your own depth-charging strategies, use the following method:

1. Estimate the depth of the deal at which you will be playing each hand. On the first hand, count the dealer's up-card, your two cards, the flashed down cards of other players at your table, and one hit card each for each player seated to your right. All subsequent rounds can be estimated by considering all the cards you will see before playing your next hand. Assume two down cards, plus one hit card for all players, including yourself, and 2.4 cards for the dealer (his up-card, his hole card, and about .4 hit cards per round).

2. Use the Complete Single-Deck Gain Table (which follows) to compose a gain table for the approach you use, employing the same methods for flat-bet, add-a-chip, double-up, etc., as I explained above. Feel free to experiment with other progression-type betting systems which could give you camouflage. Any progression will work so long as you start betting small after the shuffle and your bets get larger until the next shuffle.

You don't need to draw up your own gain tables. This methodology is presented for more advanced high stakes players, teams, etc., who want to estimate potential win rates for various creative approaches, to compare estimated win rates from different strategies.

All you must keep in mind are the important factors involved.

1. The more crowded the table, the higher your win rate, assuming you are obtaining and using the card information to play your hands.

2. The greater your edge, the larger the bets you can place, because your negative fluctuations are reduced.

3. The fewer hands you play per hour, the slower your hourly win rate.

Thus, a player with a sizeable bankroll might find depth-charging most profitable with only one or two other players at the table. A player with a small bankroll, who feels more comfortable with the possibility of less negative fluctuation, would be wise to opt for the most crowded tables he could find, and to use an outfielder, if possible. Assuming both of these players were betting the same amount, the player at the faster, less crowded tables would have an hourly expectation only slightly greater than the player at the full table.

Complete Single-Deck Gain Table

% Dealt	Cards Seen	Vegas Strip	Vegas Downtown	Northern Nevada
6	3	.00	-.20	-.50
10	5	.05	-.15	-.45
12	6	.05	-.15	-.45
15	8	.10	-.10	-.40
17	9	.15	-.05	-.35
21	11	.20	.00	-.30
23	12	.25	.05	-.25
27	14	.30	.10	-.20
29	15	.35	.15	-.15
33	17	.40	.20	-.10
35	18	.45	.25	-.05
38	20	.50	.30	.00
40	21	.55	.35	.05
44	23	.60	.40	.10
46	24	.70	.50	.20
50	26	.75	.55	.25
52	27	.80	.60	.30
56	29	.90	.70	.40
58	30	1.00	.80	.50
62	32	1.10	.90	.60
63	33	1.20	1.00	.70
67	35	1.35	1.15	.85
69	36	1.45	1.25	.95
73	38	1.65	1.45	1.15
75	39	1.75	1.55	1.25
79	41	1.95	1.75	1.45
81	42	2.20	2.00	1.70
85	44	2.60	2.40	2.10
87	45	2.90	2.70	2.40
90	47	3.70	3.50	3.20

Note: The value of depth-charging comes from accurately playing your cards at deeper and deeper shuffle points. If you do not accurately employ strategy tables to alter your play according to your count, flat-bet depth-charging is worthless. Likewise, you will realize significant gains at deep shuffle points by knowing some of the less used double-digit strategy indices for your system. I would advise depth-chargers to learn the more extensive Zen Count strategy tables provided in the Appendix. It is important that you realize that your gain comes from *seeing* and *using* as much card information as you can get, before playing your hand. Simply sitting at a full table without getting the necessary information on the other players' down cards is *not* advantageous. Red Seven Count players should not attempt to use the depth-charging gain tables to estimate win rates. These tables are for Zen Count players only.

One-Deck Wonging

One of my favorite methods of depth-charging in Reno and Tahoe is to "Wong it" in crowded single-deck games, i.e., table-hopping and playing only when the count is favorable. This is a depth-charging strategy which can be employed by both Red Seven Count players and Zen Count players. In the big casinos, I've had no trouble getting away with this strategy making single quarter ($25) bets. I've also done it with no heat betting single $20 bills. Do not expect to get away with this strategy with black ($100) chips, or stacks of quarters. High stakes players would be better off flat-betting crowded single-deck games and using an out-fielder, rather than table-hopping. Playing only one hand at a crowded table, a non-table-hopper will get about 50 hands per hour. If you cover two to three spots, you can raise your hands per hour, and thus your hourly $ win rate considerably. For low stakes players, i.e., $25 maximum bettors, this table-hopping strategy is ideal in large casinos. Smaller casinos will often give heat to $25 chip bettors.

Playing a single hand, I was able to get an average of 38 hands per hour, table-hopping crowded single-deck games, and my average edge was around 3%. I also tried playing 1 to 3 hands depending on how many spots I could grab, according to the number of players at the table and their positions. In this manner, I got about 71 hands per hour, with an edge of about 2%. I played at tables where at least 3 other players were playing, and usually there were 4 or 5 other players. One problem I encountered was not always knowing how deeply into the deck the dealer had gone. Some of my bets were met with a shuffle-up not out of dealer counter-paranoia, but because of necessity. In such cases, I played through the hands and doubled my bet size or walked on the next round, depending on the count. I never felt any heat. I did not sit down to play my hands, but stood behind the vacant seat, acting as my own outfielder. Wonging crowded single-deck games is a good approach for low-stakes players who use limited strategy tables. Using the Red Seven Count, you should be able to get about 25 to 30 hands per hour, at an average edge of about 3%, by betting only at a running count of +5 or higher. This is a potential $20 per hour. It may seem like a slow grind, but for players on limited funds, there is a wisdom to only playing hands where you enjoy such a large edge. Your negative fluctuations will be considerably reduced. Playing 25 hands per hour with a 3% edge will win at the same hourly rate as playing 75 hands per hour with a 1%

edge. After 100 hours of play with $25 bets, each approach would potentially net a win of $1,875. The player with the 3% edge, however, will have played a third as much money as the 1%-edge player, who is playing 3 times faster. The faster player with the smaller edge will need a bankroll almost twice as large as the slow player to cope with his more sizeable $ fluctuations.

Consider: If there are 5 players at a single-deck table in Reno, and you count the first round cards, you will have seen approximately 33% of the deck. A Red Seven Count of +5 would indicate a player edge of about 2½%. You will never see an edge like this after watching only one round of a 4- or 6-deck shoe game. In single-deck games, this occurs frequently. A running count of just 3 in this single-deck game with 33% depletion would indicate a full 1% player edge. You do not need to use strategy tables at all if you play only at such advantageous times. Basic strategy alone will provide a healthy long run edge over the house.

Single-deck games should be a gravy train for knowledgeable players. You have only to be able to keep a simple running count and play accurate basic strategy. Using the Red Seven Count, you have an edge over the house with *any* running count of +2 or more in single-deck games, Vegas or Reno rules. Playing multiple hands, you may be able to get more than 100 hands per hour by Wonging in on any +2 count in the big South Tahoe casinos. This is a lot of action with quarter chips. Using the Red Seven Count, the player edge is about 1% with this approach. With the Zen Count, I estimate about a 1½% edge. You can't estimate your edge with any kind of precision for this approach, because of the varying conditions—different numbers of players at the tables, various deck depletions, betting on various numbers of simultaneous hands, etc. There is no reason for a competent counter to ever play at a disadvantage in single-deck games. Whether the tables are empty or crowded, whether you've got Vegas or Reno rules, you can beat these games in the long run. The only thing I look for in single-deck games is insurance. If insurance is not offered, I take my action elsewhere.

Opposition Betting

Opposition Betting is a multi-deck betting strategy. It is especially advisable against "smart" clubs where pit bosses are liable to be watching your betting patterns. To beat multi-deck blackjack games, you must understand what you are up against. I'll be honest with you. These games are tough to beat. Many players fail to comprehend two of the most basic facts of the multi-deck challenge.

Fact 1: You cannot beat multi-deck games significantly with a flat bet or even a small spread, regardless of your system. To get a significant edge in a multi-deck game usually requires a spread of 1 to 8 units or more. The only exception to this rule would be for a table-hopper who plays only when the count is favorable. In essence, this would not be flat-betting, but using a spread in which the minimum bet is zero units. You should view table-hopping in this way because it is necessary to spend the *time* watching, counting and waiting until you can place your bets. Table-hopping is a camouflage technique which makes you appear to be a flat or small-spread bettor.

Fact 2: Multi-deck games are less vulnerable to traditional count strategies because the shifts in advantage are less volatile. Many players fail to grasp this because they do not understand the basic theory behind why card counting works. In the past year, I've received letters from otherwise knowledgeable players whose misunderstanding of this is the basis for their weak approach to beating the game. A typical such letter:

> *"On my recent trip to Vegas I played exclusively in 4-deck games. I prefer the 4-deck games because the count doesn't jump around so much. When a shoe goes hot, it often stays that way for a long-time, so I can continue to bet high for many hands in a row. In single-deck, it seems like I'll get one or two high bets then the count drops, and in no time at all they're shuffling again. In a shoe game, if the count drops real low, I leave the table and find a better game.*
>
> *"My trip was a total disaster. I couldn't have asked for better conditions, but within about 3 hours I'd lost just about my whole playing bankroll. I was spreading quarters from one-to-four, and lost $2,500. Looking back on it, the majority of my losing bets were high ($100) bets, so I guess I really only lost about 25 big bets, rather than 100 small bets. Still, I don't see how this could have happened. What's worse, almost the entire loss occurred in my last half-hour of play, against the same dealer.*
>
> *"He was dealing out about 3 decks, and every shoe the count kept climbing. By the time he'd shuffle, the running count would be between +15 and +20! Somehow I just kept losing. After three shoes like this, I was broke. I use the Hi-Lo count, so I figure that by the time he shuffled, my advantage was somewhere between 7% and 10%! It seems to me the only hand I ever played at a disadvantage was the first round after the shuffle. Then the count would go up, and it would just keep going higher. How could I lose with such hot decks?"*

This player has one glaring misconception about how card counting works. The reason that you bet high when the count is high is because your count indicates that the remaining cards contain a disproportionate number of tens and aces. You place a big bet because the odds are in your favor that these high cards will be dealt. As these cards come out of the deck, you make your money. You will be dealt more naturals. Your doubling down and pair splitting will pay off more. The dealer will bust his stiffs more frequently. You are not betting big because the count is high, per se, you are betting big that the count will come down.

If the count does not come down then this must mean that those excess high cards in the deck did not, in fact, come out. If the count continues to climb, then not only are the excess high cards not being dealt, but a disproportionate number of low cards continue to be dealt, much to your disadvantage.

If the dealer shuffles when the count is +15 to +20, then this means that all of those high cards are clumped together in the undealt portion of the shoe. If this happened three shoes in a row, then contrary to what this player's count indicated, he never had an advantage over the house. When the count *stays* high, your high bets are all for nought.

When your count goes up in a single-deck game, it is far more likely to come down than in a multi-deck game. It is this volatility that makes the one-deck games so profitable. You make your money as the count *comes down*. Ideally, you make small bets while the count is rising, and large bets as it comes back down.

Had this player been in a shoe game in which the count kept going down to about −15 to −20 prior to every shuffle, then more than likely, ironic as it may seem, this player would potentially have been able to win more money than he would have lost, since this situation would indicate that all the excess low cards were clumped in the undealt portion of the shoe.

Such a clumping of cards could occur purely through chance or possibly due to a poor shuffle. If the dealer is purposely clumping high cards, then not dealing them, this would be cheating. In any case, this is not going to be a beatable game.

First of all, in shoe games, you should always track the cutoffs. The *cutoffs* are the cards which are left in the undealt portion of the shoe. If the shuffle occurs while you have a high count, watch the shuffle. Are the cutoffs being well mixed into other cards? There are only three possibilities: *One*: The cards are being well shuffled. In this case, you're getting a fair deal. If, however, your cutoff count is *always* high, I would advise finding a new table. There's a possibility that you're being cheated by an expert, so don't take that risk. *Possibility Two:* The cutoffs are not being well-mixed with the other cards, and in fact, end up being cut off again. Whether this is due to chance or design, get out of the game. *Possibility Three:* The cutoffs are not being well-mixed, but this time end up clumped in the playable portion of the deck. Don't leave the table. You know where the high cards are so play and bet accordingly. If the cutoffs are mixed into only half of the shoe, then bet high in this half. Play all cards in this portion of the shoe as if your count were high. Depending on what the cutoff count was before the shuffle, and on the portion of the shoe into which the cutoffs were mixed, approximate a running count for this entire portion of the shoe, and play this portion by starting your count at that level. Use the reverse strategy if the cutoff count is very low and the cutoffs are not well mixed.

I first learned this trick from Lance Humble's *Blackjack Supergold* (page 94). Humble advises using your knowledge of the deck composition after the shuffle to cut the high card portion of the deck to the top, thus allowing you to bet high off the top. If you are fortunate enough to be offered the cut, this would definitely be the way to do it for maximum camouflage. But you can take advantage of the shoe even if another player cuts, so long as the high cards are not cut out of play.

Humble notes that in the 4-deck Vegas game, it is common for the cutoff portion to be about one deck, and it is also common for this portion to be mixed into a similar-sized portion, but not into the entire shoe. In this case, the cutoffs are all confined to a two-deck portion, or about one half of the shoe. To approximate the running count for this half-deck portion, you subtract one third of your cutoff running count. It makes no difference whether your cutoff count is plus or minus, since the other half of the shoe is simply the same count with the opposite sign.

For example, if your cutoff running count is +12, subtract exactly one third of this (+4). Your *starting* running count for this two-deck portion is +8. Play this portion of the shoe as if you are in a two-deck game. If you are using the Red Seven Count, your two-deck pivot is +4, so you may bet high through much of these two decks. With the Zen Count, make your true count adjustments as if you were in a two-deck game.

I have observed this sloppy shuffle technique in major casinos in both Las Vegas and Northern Nevada. When you are looking for a table to play, watch for dealers who are near the ends of their shoes. When a shuffle occurs, track the cutoffs. When you find a dealer whose cutoffs can be tracked, stick with him.

This is one situation where *opposition betting* can make you some money. While you are playing in the high-card portion of the shoe, a disproportionate number of high cards will be dealt. To the dealer, pit boss, or eye upstairs, it appears that the count is continually going down. As this occurs, your best strategy is to continue raising your bet. Your bet sizing will appear to be in direct opposition to the betting strategy a card counter would employ. Similarly, when you are playing in the low-card portion of the shoe, your count appears to be steadily on the rise. Your strategy here will be the opposite. Steadily lower your bets down to the table minimum.

You do not need to play against dealers who can't shuffle in order to use opposition betting in shoe games. I first learned of this strategy from various old-timers who had independently developed opposition betting strategies which were technically different styles, but essentially had the same effect.

Opposition betting is sizing your bets so as to appear to be raising your bets when the count is going down and lowering your bets when the count is going up. The purpose of opposition betting is to get a large spread. The following is an explanation of how one Vegas pro gets away with it; I've paraphrased his words, and changed enough details to protect his identity:

"I've been playing blackjack for thirty years. For about the first twenty I didn't know anything about counting. At one point I tried to read Thorp's book, but the system was beyond me. Revere's book became my bible because his point count system was powerful and so much easier. I still use it. By the time I'd started counting, I was well known in the casinos as a high roller. I was comped most everywhere, and still am. My basic method of camouflage, once I'd started counting, was simply to keep playing as much as possible the way I'd always played.

"I buy in at the craps table and usually spend my first ten or fifteen minutes playing craps for nickels. I'll often get a whole rack of chips—half quarters, half nickels. I never hide chips, or pocket chips, or try to look like I'm losing. I never did that before I was a counter, so why should I start now? Whether you're counting or not sometimes you win, sometimes you lose. When I lose a lot, I sulk around the pit till I get a room. I make a lot of noise about it when I win big. The only time I pocket chips is when I cash out. I'll go south with one or two blacks, and play them in the next casino.

"When I hit the blackjack tables, I start betting with nickels—two or three at a time. If the count starts going down, I'll bet even bigger—four or five nickels. If it keeps going down, I might push six to eight of them out there. As the count goes up, I use the reverse strategy. I'll go down to a single nickel and keep betting this way until my true count gets up around +6. Sometimes I'll go through a couple shoes till I get a count like this. Sometimes it happens right away. But when it does go up that high, I'll raise my bet from a single nickel to a stack of quarters in one jump. I'll just throw eight of 'em on the table like that. By this time, I'm already pegged as a non-counter because of all my stupid bets before. And if they don't have me pegged this way, they will soon. My strategy with the quarters is pretty much the same as my nickel strategy. If the count goes up, I just let my stack of quarters ride. While the count is this high, I make sure I've got a couple hundred bucks on the table. It's important to me not to raise my bet if the count goes up even higher. You see, I start raising it when the count's coming back down. Dealers always change colors on you when you bet stacks of chips. If I win with eight quarters, he'll pay me off with a couple of blacks. The next stack of chips I'll push out there will have those blacks on the bottom. By the time my true count is down to +3 or so, I'll be making bets of $500 to $600. I'd say my average high bet is about $250 to $350. My average low bet is probably about $15 to $20.

"About the only time I might be suspected of counting is when I make my jump from a nickel to a couple hundred bucks. Before and after that, I usually raise and lower my bets in reverse.

"I make a lot of money using this method. It's not a cut-and-dried approach. A lot of times I'll jump my bets around according to whether I'm winning or losing. Often I mix up my colors and have reds, greens and blacks in the same stack. It drives dealers nuts. Part of my method is to look like I just don't have much of a method. Sometimes I bet high off the top of the shoe. For the most part, I play nickels with low counts and greens and blacks with high counts. When I make my big jump, I wait until the time seems right for it. If the count is high, and I've only got a nickel riding on the bet, I'm likely to split fours or fives, or maybe stand on a twelve against a ten. After a play like that, dealers love to see you start playing with real money. You see, they know I've got the greens and blacks. I'm sitting there with half a rack of them in front of me. I don't make foolish plays when I'm betting big, though.

"I've watched dozens of counters get 86'd. Most of them are young. They always spread from one to four. They're so easy to spot it's laughable. Sometimes I think my best camouflage is that I'm old and bald. My second best camouflage might be that I've got a lot of money. Counters look hungry. There's probably not much a young guy can do about this, but still, he *can* change his one-to-four spread to something that looks less intelligent. All the books say spread from 1 to 4 or 1 to 8. There's not a pit boss in Vegas who hasn't read most of these books. When you play like the books say, you're advertising your smarts.

"One time I was sitting with two counters for about half an hour. During the course of that half hour, I'd placed bets as low as a nickel and as high as seven or eight hundred bucks. They were both spreading quarters from one-to-four. They kept nudging each other when I'd make a stupid play. Once I insured my natural at a low count. I had two nickels on the table. Then the true count went up to about +9 or +10 real fast. I hit my four card sixteen against the dealer's five and busted. I had a nickel riding on it. Both of them did everything they could to contain themselves. I mumbled something about how I could feel a hot streak coming and pushed out a stack of greens and blacks—mostly blacks. It must have been close to a thousand bucks. I guess these guys got brave then because both of them raised their next bets to eight chips. Frankly, I was having a hard time not laughing, myself. Their bets had been so identical since they'd sat down they were like the Bobbsey Twins.

"The pit boss jumped in at that point. He went through the discards and politely told these two guys to hit the road. They were upset. One of them remarked that it should be illegal for casinos to only deal to stupid players. The remark was directed at me. They ended up getting barred.

"I don't want you to think I never get any heat. There are a few casinos in this town I won't set foot in. But I've got an excellent rating at most of the places that matter, dating back to the sixties. I'm welcome at most of the Atlantic City casinos. I had a little trouble with a pit boss in one A.C. joint. You can't fool everybody... But I've made quite a bit of money in A.C., so I can't knock it."

This is a crude approach to opposition betting but it illustrates the basic camouflage techniques. Without an enormous spread, such as this player employs, you could not win much money with such a drastic betting style.

The opposition bettor wins money by getting away with a large spread. Over any extended period of play, his betting looks foolish from a card counter's perspective. This is not a cut-and-dried approach to betting. One highly successful player told me he never placed more than four chips on the table at a time, and never less than two. He mixed his colors to get a big spread, and used the same technique of playing and betting more "stupidly" at low counts. Most of his changes in bet size were opposition bets, and he got his spread with sudden big jumps.

I tried a variation of opposition betting using $2, $5, and $25 chips in Las Vegas, and got no heat in an hour and a half of play at each of two large casinos. I spread from $2 to $55 (two quarters capped with a nickel, since one opposition bettor explained that he feels it's important to never bet big chips only, even in a small stack). This was admittedly a short test, and was not for high stakes, but I could not have imagined getting away with this spread so blatantly otherwise.

Another highly effective opposition betting technique is one developed by Ralph Stricker, who operates a school for blackjack players on the East Coast. My east coast newsletter correspondent, math-whiz Bob Fisher, wrote a program to test Stricker's approach to the 6-deck Atlantic City game, by computer simulation. The preliminary runs indicate this approach to be highly advantageous.

I think it's important to remember that there is not *one* method of opposition betting. It's a camouflage technique that can be used any number of ways. Based on Stricker's method, which is one of the most sophisticated opposition betting strategies I've encountered, I'll present here a method I devised and tested at the tables, and I'll urge you to devise your own method—which is not difficult once you understand the principles involved.

Stricker bases his betting approach on the fact that in multi-deck games, neither the house nor the player has any significant edge for most of the game. The player may take advantage, in the form of camouflage bet-sizing, during these long periods of play when there is no significant advantage for either side. As a counter, you can make the majority of your changes in bet size appear to be either haphazard, or based on some non-counting progression-type system. Stricker reports that he and his students have had phenomenal success in the 6-deck Atlantic City games, using a progression-type system through the "neutral" counts, yet actually spreading from 1 to 10 when the edge was significant one way or the other.

To test the feasibility of this approach in Nevada, I tried my own method, using the Zen Count in 4-deck Strip games. At true counts of 0 through +4, my advantage runs from about −½% to +½%. At all negative counts the house has greater than a ½% edge over me. At all true counts of greater than +4, I have an advantage of greater than ½% over the house.

This is how I bet: At all negative counts I bet one nickel. At all true counts from 0 through +4, I alternate my bets. First I bet a nickel, then I bet a quarter capped with a nickel. Then a nickel, etc. I do this regardless of whether the count is rising or falling. When the count is greater than +4, I bet two quarters capped with a nickel.

The advantage from betting in this manner is close to what my advantage would be if I were simply and without camouflage jumping my bets from $5 to $55. Yet when I tried this betting technique in three Vegas casinos, my high bets never raised an eyebrow. By the time I'd made my first high bet, I was halfway into the shoe and had been alternating high-low-high-low for quite a few hands. It looks like a worthless progression because it is one. My true count hit +5 so I followed my low $5 bet with a $55 high bet that was simply one chip higher than my normal $30 high bet. I let this bet ride until the count went down to +3, then went back to my alternating high-low bets.

There are as many approaches to opposition betting as there are progression type systems. I won't recommend any one approach because I feel it's important that you never look like you're playing "by the book." How much of a spread you can get with this approach is limited by your personal bankroll, the house table limits, and the number of decks in play.

You cannot practically use opposition betting tactics in single-deck games. My experience with attempting it was that too often, by the time I made my camouflage bet, either the count changed too radically, or the shuffle occurred. You may have noted, however, that in its "pure" add-a-chip or double-up forms, depth-charging is technically an opposition betting strategy. In games of four or more decks, opposition betting takes advantage of a factor that would ordinarily make counting ineffective—the slow volatility of the edge. A player with a sufficient bankroll to play house limits may find multi-deck games more profitable than single-deck games.

One drawback to opposition betting: Your bankroll fluctuations will be sizeable. It takes a healthy bankroll to use any large spread, because of the size of your high bets. You cannot use opposition betting tactics with a small spread. Your camouflage bets will nullify profit potential.

Some cautions: Be careful with "stupid" looking camouflage plays. Unless you're using a *very* large spread, don't make really ridiculous plays like splitting fours or fives. Also, always restrict your stupid plays to your lowest bets. These should be occasional plays only, and well timed for maximum camouflage effect.

Many players use the terms "hot" shoe or "cold" shoe. Too often, players misuse these slang terms because of their misunderstanding of how counting works. Definition: *a hot shoe* is a shoe with a great *fluctuation* in advantage. Specifically, the count goes up, then comes down, then goes up, then down, etc. A *cold shoe* is one with little fluctuation, regardless of whether the count stays neutral, continuously climbs, or steadily falls through the shoe. A continuously falling count could be advantageous since so many high cards are being dealt, but you will realize small profits from such shoes. Your bet size will likely be small, and you will be playing your hands as if the count were low. Most shoes are neither cold nor hot, but somewhere between cool and lukewarm. This is where opposition betting shows its power.

Opposition betting in multi-deck games is similar to depth-charging in single-deck games. What you are doing is *invisibly* turning the volatility of the edge to your favor. Since the volatility is diminished in multi-deck games, it's necessary to use a large spread. But the slow volatility allows you increased camouflage betting tactics. Keep in mind that the more camouflage you use, the more you will actually hurt your win rate. For this reason, the Stricker approach strikes me as the most advantageous. Use a stupid progression when the edge is about neutral. Bet one unit when the house has the edge, and bet whatever your bankroll can afford when you have the edge. The slow volatility of the game makes possible all the camouflage you need. In the Zen Count example described earlier, consider how this approach would appear in the 6-deck Atlantic City game, with a two-deck shuffle-point. Approximately 43% of my hands would be played with a one-chip bet, because that is how often my count would be below 0. About 45% of my bets would be played with alternating nickel then nickel-quarter bets, because that is how often the Zen Count player would be playing hands at true counts ranging from 0 to +4. About 12% of my bets would be high (nickel-quarter-quarter) bets, because that is how often my true count would be above +4. By the time this high bet is made, I would be firmly established as a progression-type bettor. My limited 4-deck Vegas experience revealed to me the validity of this approach as an effective camouflage technique. Try it, and you'll realize immediately why it works. For most of my play, if I were sitting next to a player who was using my betting approach, I would not guess him to be a counter. Neither will the casinos. It would often require *hours* of personal observation to identify an opposition bettor with any degree of certainty. For this reason, opposition betting is one of the best approaches to games where a large spread is *necessary* to obtain a significant edge over the house.

High stakes opposition bettors tell me that the best progression-type systems to use for camouflage purposes are the typical gamblers' progressions. Either parlay your wins by adding chips, doubling up, etc., or chase your losses in a similarly predictable fashion, throughout neutral portions of the shoe.

With a moderate 1-to-4 spread, a 6-deck game is not worth much more than about .2% to a card counter who sits through the negative shoes. It you quit the table at negative counts, an opposition bet-jumping 1-to-11 spread, as described above, will make this game worth about .6%. If you make it a practice to seek out games with shuffle points of between one and one-and-one-half decks, you should be able to get close to a 1% edge in 6-deck games, using this betting style. You'll look less like a counter. You'll significantly raise your expected return. If you get your spread by lowering your low bet rather than by raising your high bet you'll also be able to decrease your bankroll fluctuations.

For instance, if you currently spread from $25 to $100, try opposition betting with a spread from $5 to $100. Perhaps bet a nickel on low negative counts; use a haphazard $5 to $75 on relatively "neutral" counts. And jump to $105 on high counts. Not only would you triple your potential win rate, you'd noticeably cut your bankroll fluctuations. Using such a large spread is similar to table-hopping in that the vast majority of your serious money bets are at high counts.

For multi-deck games, opposition betting strikes me as the most profitable and practical way to play. In a nutshell:

1. In multi-deck games, almost half of your hands are played when neither you nor the dealer has any significant edge.

2. During these "neutral" hands, a good card counter would break even if he were flat-betting.

3. Betting progression type systems are not detrimental to your advantage, they are merely worthless, i.e., they will not affect your basically break-even game one way or the other.

4. During these neutral hands, therefore, you may bet like a complete fool, in order to establish this image for the dealer, pit boss, etc.

5. Card counters are generally suspected and identified by their betting styles, not how they play their hands. Don't overdo "stupid" camouflage plays. Most of the time, you will not need such plays to camouflage your counting. Your seemingly foolish betting is your best camouflage. If you do make an occasional "stupid" play, do it only when your bet is small.

To come back to the analogy of the martial arts master: The master spends much time launching false attacks on his opponent, though he is merely waiting for his opponent to be off balance. The opponent gains much confidence during the master's waiting period, because the master's false attacks are so impotent. When the opponent loses his balance, as he will, even his perspective is unstable. He does not see the actual attack of the master.

And isn't this how a pool hustler works? And isn't this how a professional poker player operates? And a chess grandmaster? Card counting is a science. Beating the casinos at blackjack is something else again. It is an art.

IDIOT CAMOUFLAGE

Camouflage is a military term that means disguise. A soldier has a better chance at survival if he looks like the rest of the jungle. For a card counter, camouflage means essentially the same thing. It's an act that pegs you as Ted Tourist or Harry Highroller or Donald Drunk—anyone but Clyde Counter.

There are many aspects to camouflage. Physical camouflage, such as a false beard, is not needed by most counters. Unless you're a *known* counter, this would be a waste of time. In Chapters Nine and Ten, various types of betting camouflage were described. There is a *dramatic* camouflage that most successful players find to be as important as card counting when it comes to being a consistent winner. Dramatic camouflage would include such subtle touches as appearing uninterested in other players' cards or being preoccupied with idle table chatter. It would include the ability to raise bets as if chasing losses, or as if you believe you are on a winning streak. This dramatic camouflage is probably the single most difficult aspect of card counting for a player to learn. Some people are born actors; most people aren't. Show me a successful card counter and I'll show you a person who has all the innate abilities of the con artist.

One type of camouflage which many players use, often because they lack the subtle skills of the dramatic camouflage expert, is *idiot* camouflage.

As you might suspect, idiot camouflage is making a stupid play. If the pit boss starts watching you suspiciously, you play like an idiot. You split a pair of fives against a dealer's ace, then you stand on your hard total of 11 (versus anything!). This, of course, looks so idiotic that the pit boss soon turns away, his counter-paranoia having totally disappeared. Now you can do whatever you want for the next hour and get rich.

Or, at least, that's the way idiot camouflage is supposed to work. Unfortunately, what usually happens is that ten minutes later, a new pit boss comes by, or the dealers change, or you start to wonder about the eye upstairs, so you have to make another idiot play or two.

If you have not been blessed with acting talents, you may tend to overcompensate for this drawback by sprinkling your play with substantial amounts of idiot camouflage. Idiot camouflage has one thing in its favor: *it's easy*. It has one thing going against it: *it's costly*.

The counter's edge is small. It doesn't take many stupid plays to wipe out your profit potential. If you're not a born actor, and you feel that idiot camouflage is what keeps you in the game, here are some guidelines:

1. Reserve your stupid plays for your smallest bets.
If you've got big money on the table, this is the wrong time to try to look dumb. If you're using a 1-to-8 spread, the same stupid play could cost you eight times more money when you have a high bet out.

2. Use a stupid play only when you feel it is necessary.
Don't try to prove to every dealer you sit down against that you're no threat. Most dealers don't pay any attention to how you're playing. They watch players all day long, and they're bored stiff with the game. Try to make small talk if you can.

3. Pair-Splitting Camouflage
Don't make stupid pair-split decisions. You're doubling your money on the table when most dealers don't know correct pair-splitting basic strategy anyway. Occasionally, you'll have a very high count and a pair of tens vs. a dealer low card. The Zen Count may indicate that you should split your tens. This is one pair split hand you might consider playing incorrectly, and likewise is one of the few hands you might consider playing incorrectly when you have a high bet on the table. Splitting ten-valued cards is an unusual play for both stupid and smart players. Few players break up a hand totaling 20. Without dramatic camouflage, this play usually looks suspicious. If you've been playing an otherwise intelligent game, this could look very suspicious.

If you've got a small bet on the table, you might occasionally consider splitting a pair of threes vs. an ace. This happens to be a hand where the stupid-looking play won't cost you much. Likewise, if you use the Zen Count, you would be making a technically correct play if you split a pair of nines vs. an ace, if your true count is +7 or higher. You won't make much money from this play, but it is correct, and it looks dumb.

4. Double-Down Camouflage

Don't make stupid double-down decisions, especially on hard totals. Again, twice the money is involved. If you hit your 11 against a dealer 5, instead of doubling down, the dealer could care less, and you just blew a good chance to make some money. Most tourists double down on 11. Most non-counters are ignorant, however, of soft doubling rules, and because of this, doubling correctly on some soft hands may draw attention to you as an intelligent player. Few unskilled players ever double down on A-2, A-3, A-4 or A-5. You won't lose much by hitting these hands instead of doubling, barely more than one twentieth of a percent loss if you *never* doubled on any of them. With these hands, idiot camouflage doesn't hurt you much.

5. Standing Camouflage

Don't *stand* on your A-2, A-3, A-4 or A-5. It's not costly to ignore the soft doubling strategy for these hands, but *always* hit these soft hands. Follow your Stand decisions correctly. Stupid plays here can cost plenty. One Stand decision you might play wrong, without much of a loss, occurs when you have a pair of sevens vs. a dealer ten in a single-deck game. This is, of course, that one weird total of 14 where the correct basic strategy is to stand, rather than hit. Unfortunately, just about every blackjack book (other than this one!) since Thorp's *Beat the Dealer* has explained this in detail. It's a play that smart players make, and many pit personnel know it. It's actually a borderline basic strategy play. You won't lose much by hitting your 7-7 vs. 10. Likewise, if you're using the complete Zen Count tables from the Appendix, you might find it occasionally "correct" to hit a hard 17 vs. a dealer ace. I advise against ever hitting a hard 17, unless you've got an incredible drunk act.

6. Insurance Camouflage

As for insurance, casinos like to tell players two "good" rules; first, always insure a natural; second, always insure a "good" hand. The first rule is fine. You'll only lose about one hundredth of a percent over the long run if you always insure your naturals. You'll definitely be noticed if you don't insure your naturals. But don't always insure your "good" hands. This would be far more costly, and it's not really necessary for camouflage purposes.

7. Correct Play Camouflage

Zen Count players might occasionally take advantage of some other technically correct plays, which are not worth much, except as camouflage. If your true count is higher than +11, don't split a pair of 8's vs. a dealer X. If it's below −10, don't split your aces vs. an ace. If it's below −15, don't split aces vs. 8, 9, or X. All of these plays are correct, but they look dumb because smart players always split aces and 8's, and the casinos know it.

Make a bad play only when you feel it will be effective for maximum camouflage value. Don't make any bad plays as a rule. There's no real difference between a player who uses constant idiot camouflage ... and a real idiot.

♣♦♠♥

TOKING GUIDELINES

"Toking" is casino slang for tipping. A knowledgeable blackjack player tokes the dealer either to maintain good playing conditions or to obtain better conditions. Overtipping can nullify the potential profit from card counting. Tokes may be categorized as either *general* or *specific*.

General Tokes

A *general* toke is a toke made to maintain or improve the player's long-run playing conditions. Placing a bet for the dealer shortly after beginning play, in hopes of favorably influencing the dealer, is an example of a general toke. This dealer may be less suspicious, more apt to deal lower into the deck, and more likely to ignore a betting spread. Tips made solely for the purpose of camouflage, in order to give the appearance of a high roller, would also fall into the category of general tokes. This type of tipping is recommended by Ian Andersen in *Turning the Tables on Las Vegas*.

To avoid general toking in excess of one's profit potential, a player must realistically consider his expected average hourly profit, based on hands per hour, average bet size, and approximate advantage over the house. The expected hourly win is estimated by using the Profit Formula, from Chapter Five. Example: An average bet of $50, at 120 hands per hour, with a long-run advantage over the house of 1% from card counting:

$$\text{Expected hourly win} = \$50 \times 120 \times .01 = \$60.$$

From this expectation the player may decide how much he wishes to "give back" to the dealer in tokes. A frequent error of rookie card counters is to toke excessively.

Many times I have seen a player betting quarters, using a moderate spread, and playing a solid game, suddenly toss a $25 chip to the dealer because the player had a lucky 20-minute run, and won a few hundred dollars. Paying a dealer so lavishly for a winning streak is a sure road to the poor house. Winning streaks occur frequently, and to toke after every one is expensive. Losing streaks occur just as frequently, though I have yet to see a dealer toke a player who has just lost a few hundred dollars. Toking after a win should be classified as a general toke. The size and frequency of such tokes should be calculated according to long-run expectations.

If playing head-on with the dealer, a player will average about 200 hands per hour. When at a crowded table one will rarely play more than 70 hands per hour. If playing head-on, therefore, you would expect an hourly profit three times that of playing at a full table, assuming the same average bet size and the same advantage over the house. Likewise, a head-on player with only one-third of the average bet of a full-table player would enjoy the same hourly profit potential, if both were playing with the same long-run advantage.

Let's assume the player enjoys a long-run advantage of 1% over the house, with an average bet size of $100. In a head-on game, this player would expect a profit of about $200 per hour. If the player is toking flamboyantly as a camouflage, he may toss out a $25 chip every hour, or half a dozen $5 chips per hour, without seriously cutting into potential profits. At a full table, however, this player's expectation is not more than $70 per hour. A $25 toke in this game every hour represents a sizeable portion of his total expectation. (I am assuming here that the full-table player still enjoys a 1% advantage over the house. Full tables may also cut into profits by reducing the percentage of the cards dealt out, and by reducing a player's betting accuracy.)

Consider a six-deck game, where a table-hopper with a moderate betting spread enjoys an advantage of about 1%. With crowded tables and limited play, a $100 average bet will yield an expectation of only about $60 per hour, with 60 hands per hour. Any sizeable toking in this game should be done by players who are making average bets of $400 to $500. Players making $25 average bets would be unwise to toke at all under such conditions, as their expected rate of profit would only be about $15 per hour. Since less crowded playing conditions could triple your potential hands per hour, some games with less favorable rules might be more profitable on an hourly basis, justifying more lavish tipping.

You must be realistic in estimating your hourly win rate. It would be wise to estimate total toke-dollars as a per-hour average, based on how much of your potential win you feel should be reinvested, either for camouflage purposes, or otherwise. Tips to cocktail waitresses, and *any other expenses* incurred in casino play should also be considered from this perspective.

Specific Tokes

Specific toking is toking for an immediate potential gain. Toking a dealer in an effort to influence him to deal one more round before shuffling at a high count is a specific toke. The size of the toke must be determined on the basis of the potential gain from one specific hand. Player advantage from card counting rarely exceeds 3% on a high count, and in most multi-deck games, an advantage over 2% is uncommon. Players who make specific tokes should closely monitor results. How often does a bet placed for a dealer fail to influence his action? If a dealer does not *suspect* you of counting cards, he may shuffle anyway, unaware of the toke's purpose. With a 2% advantage, a single hand would profit you $2 for every $100 you bet. Toking the dealer $1 for every $100 bet would split the profit 50-50 between you and the dealer. Toking the dealer $5 for a $100 bet would be giving him more than twice your expectation.

A bet placed for the dealer by a player hoping to read a tell (Chapter Thirteen) is another example of specific toking. Some dealers are easy to read only when a toke is riding on the outcome. Here again, a player must not pay more for the tell than the tell is worth.

Stanford Wong, in *Winning Without Counting* (see Appendix), has determined the player advantage from a *reliable* and *accurate* tell to be about 2%. If you were in a 4-deck Vegas game, or a single-deck Reno game, where the basic strategy starting advantage is about $-\frac{1}{2}$%, a good tell would be worth only about $1\frac{1}{2}$% of the money you bet on any given hand. In such a game, if you knew with certainty that the dealer would unconsciously reveal whether or not he was pat or stiff (if and only if he checks his hole card), the tell information would potentially profit you about $1.50 for every $100 you bet for yourself. If you are toking $1 with a $100 bet, you would potentially be profiting only 50¢ on this hand. This is impractical as a consistent method of play. It is a dangerous practice to throw money on the table for the dealer hand after hand, and especially dangerous if you are both winning! The dealer may be unconscious of his tell, but the house will not be unconscious of it for long. A good tell player may provide an occasional general toke—*only if the dealer's favorable disposition encourages the tell beyond the specific toked hand.*

Specific toking is of no practical value to most players. General toking, as part of an act, may occasionally be useful. Such toking should be carefully planned to increase profits, not eat them. Card counters making average bets of less than $25 should not toke at all.

HOLE CARD PLAY

Hole card play refers to any strategy in which you base your playing decisions on knowledge of the dealer's hole card. Unless you connect with a full-time professional blackjack team, you will probably not be able to gain much from hole card play. Opportunities for the various hole card strategies come few and far between, and avail themselves most often to pros who have the time to seek them out and take advantage of them. In **Atlantic City, hole card play is impossible since the dealer does not check his second card until** all players have completed playing their hands.

Playing Warps

Occasionally you will spot a deck which has been in use for an extended period of time, and in which many of the cards are slightly bent, or warped. Usually, this will mean nothing, but occasionally, the warps will be "readable."

When the dealer has an ace or a ten up, he must check his hole card to see if he has a blackjack. In doing so, he will usually bend the ace or ten upwards so that he can peek at his hole card. If the dealer does this continually over a long period of time, he will sometimes end up with a deck of cards in which a sizeable proportion of aces and tens will form slight arches if laid face down on a table. When a deck is badly warped in this way, you will be able to see the arch of such a card when it is lying beneath the dealer's up card.

The majority of the profit from being able to read warps comes from taking or declining insurance when the dealer has an ace up. You should not attempt to use warps for insurance decisions unless you first determine that you can predict the dealer's hole card, as being either a ten/ace or a non-ten/ace, with a high degree of accuracy. I advise against attempting to use warp information for other playing strategy decisions since the gains are small.

Spooking

Spooking is catching a glimpse of the dealer's hole card when the dealer checks for a natural. Spooking is usually done by partners, and sometimes by whole teams of players. One person, the spook, usually must be positioned behind the dealer in order to be able to see the hole card when the dealer peeks at it. The spook must then pass the information by inconspicuous signals to the player in time for the player to make a decision based on this information. It is often necessary to use relays between the spook and the player. Most dealers are not spookable.

Occasionally, you may discover a dealer who is spookable from first base, if he has a high roller on the third base side of the table. Such a dealer, in his efforts to conceal his hole card from the big money player, may inadvertently expose his hole cards to the first base player, by lifting it in the first base direction. Most dealers will not be this sloppy. The best way to take advantage of such a dealer is for a pair of players, one betting big at third base, the other betting small at first base. The first base player can then signal the third base player whether the dealer is pat or stiff. I know one nickel bettor who lives in Reno, who keeps a file on dealers who are spookable from first base. It's a small list, compiled over many years. He does not work in collusion with big players, but simply looks for high rollers playing the third base side of the table vs. first-base-spookable dealers. He then sits at first base and makes $10 to $20 bets, simply using the hole card information for himself.

Whenever you are using hole card information, you must do so conservatively. For instance, just because you know the dealer has a 20 doesn't mean you should hit your hard 17. To do this draws too much attention to yourself. You're more likely to use hole card information for playing your stiffs. If the dealer has a ten up, but you know he has a 6 in the hole, you would stand on your hard 12. This would make you look stupid, and it would also be the correct play.

Unless you get heavily involved in the Nevada card-counting subculture, you are unlikely to have much use for spooking. But it doesn't hurt to keep your eyes open when you are playing first base, especially when there's a high roller on the other end of the table.

Front Loading

A front loader is a dealer who inadvertently flashes his hole card to the player(s) while he is placing it beneath his up-card. Front loading is also used as a verb which means glimpsing the dealer's hole card, again, while he is initially sliding it beneath his up-card. Few dealers are consistent front loaders. Professional blackjack teams spend weeks casing casinos just to find one or two such dealers. Every once in a while, I get a letter from a "tourist" player who has accidentally discovered a front loader. Your advantage over the house when playing against such a dealer is large, so you must employ a conservative strategy, to keep the house from getting suspicious. Confine your weird plays to playing your stiffs correctly, and never doubling down or splitting pairs if the dealer has an 18 or higher.

Again, unless you become a full-time card counter, you are unlikely to have much use for front loading. Like spooking, front loading is done best by partners and teams with relays, signals, etc. If you happen to sit down across from a dealer who is so sloppy he inadvertently flashes his hole card, you will find it profitable to play against him. The main reason you cannot make such plays as hitting hard 17 when the dealer has 18 is that the house may believe that you are colluding with the dealer. You could both be arrested for cheating. Keep this in mind any time you play hole cards.

Playing Tells

A tell is a readable pattern of behavior. The term is common among poker players, whose success depends on their ability to read the strength of their opponents' hands. Some blackjack dealers have tells that are exhibited when they check their hole cards. Some slight mannerism, or facial expression, will tip off the perceptive player as to whether the dealer is pat or stiff. Playing tells is an art. Most players that I know, including most full-time professional card counters, are unable to recognize dependable tells, in spite of years of attempts. Those few players who have the ability to play tells seem unable to explain exactly how they discover tells. Tell players admit to spending many hours studying a single dealer in search of a readable tell, usually in vain. When a reliable tell is discovered, it is often only a temporary mannerism, that is present when the dealer is in a particular mood or frame of mind. Unless you live in Nevada, I doubt you will have the time to develop tell playing into a profitable occupation. But it is fun to look for tells, especially when games are crowded and table conditions are otherwise poor for card counting. Watch for any change in a dealer's face at the moment he checks his hole card. If you notice any facial change whatsoever, wait to see whether the dealer was pat or stiff. Continue to study the dealer in this way in search of a predictable pattern. If you find no reliable tells after a while, move to the next table. You will occasionally find dealers with semi-reliable tells, and you may be tempted to play. Remember that unless you are naturally talented at reading tells, playing tells is risky. Playing a "semi-reliable" tell is not much better than playing a hunch.

105

DEALERS WHO CHEAT 14

Cheating does exist in casinos. Unfortunately, there is little the player can do to protect himself, except walk away from any table where he suspects he is being cheated. Players who are playing for low stakes, up to $5 chips, will be less likely to be cheated than high stakes players. Players in single or double-deck hand held games will be more likely to be cheated than players in shoe games. Players at crowded tables will be less likely to be cheated than players in head-to-head games.

Blackjack pros and card sharps agree that most casino blackjack dealers are honest. Blackjack pros know this because they continue to profit from high stakes card counting year after year. If cheating dealers were common, this would be impossible. Card sharps are among the few who can recognize cheating moves. Most card sharps will tell you that you have to be able to perform many of the cheating moves yourself in order to recognize them. They will also tell you that some of the most common cheating methods are not detectable by *anyone*.

In September of 1982, at one of the major Strip casinos in Las Vegas, a woman sitting in the first base seat at one of the blackjack tables noticed something curious. The dealer, in sliding a card from the 6-deck shoe on the table, accidentally nudged the shoe a fraction of an inch, slightly exposing the edge of what appeared to be a card lying beneath the shoe. The woman, somewhat taken aback by this discovery, reached out and lifted the shoe from the table, exposing the card, which had been lying face down beneath the shoe. She turned the card up. It was an ace. It had been positioned beneath the shoe in such a way that the dealer could have inconspicuously nudged the shoe back a fraction of an inch to facilitate sliding the card out from beneath the shoe, as if dealing the card from the shoe in a normal fashion.

Aces do not accidentally fall beneath dealing shoes. Someone had plans for that ace.

Sliding a hidden card from beneath a dealing shoe is probably not a common cheating technique because of the many difficulties this move presents. First of all, someone must inconspicuously hide the card in the first place. Secondly, if the card is detected prior to its being used, the dealer would be suspect. There is no natural way for a card to get into that position. I mention this particular cheating method, not because I think you should start picking up shoes to look for hidden cards before playing, but because, to my knowledge, this was the first instance of this cheating method ever having been exposed. Dealing shoes have been used for decades. Yet some of the most knowledgeable card sharps I spoke with had never heard of this gaff.

A talented card cheat would not perform any detectable moves, and would not resort to any device which could be used as evidence, if discovered—such as hidden cards, marked cards, etc. If he stacks the deck, performs false shuffles, peaks at the top card, or deals the second card from the top, all of these movements will appear natural. Unless you have personally witnessed close-up demonstrations of these techniques by expert card manipulators, you would be amazed at some of the "miracles" a sleight-of-hand artist can perform with a standard deck of playing cards.

There are only a few basic warning signals that are easy for the player to detect in attempting to avoid cheating dealers. Probably the easiest, least detectable, and, hence, most common cheating technique is simply to make incorrect payoffs. Always pay attention to the amount you have bet, and the amount of your payoff. Especially, watch for incorrect payoffs on blackjacks and insurance bets. If a hand occurs where you or the dealer, or both, take many small hit cards, be sure you add up the totals of both hands. If the dealer collects your money before you finish adding, stop him. Make sure all payoffs are correct. You'll get faster at this as you gain experience.

A false shuffle is a difficult cheating move to detect. It may be used in either single- or multi-deck games. No sleight-of-hand is necessary for this move. The dealer simply locates a clump of high cards by noting their approximate position when he places them in the discard tray (or his hand, if single-deck). Then, when later shuffling the cards, he controls this clump and positions it where it will be cut out of play.

No other sleight or move is necessary. A shuffle of this type is undetectable to players, pit bosses, and the Eye in the Sky. Yet, the dealer will completely nullify any potential gain from card counting, and over the long run, will win a greater amount of money from all the players who play against him.

This type of cheating is particularly devastating to card counters because it causes the count to continually go up as the excess low cards are dealt. The counter raises his bets, but the expected high cards never come out.

The easiest way to handle this type of cheating is to leave the table.

Your only clue that this false shuffle technique is being used will be that you will notice the count is always high when the dealer shuffles. If this occurs frequently, leave the table. (Note: Chapter Ten explains an advanced method whereby you might turn this cheating technique to *your* advantage.)

The second warning signal that you are being cheated also involves a false shuffle. Again, the mechanics of the shuffle will be undetectable, but the result of the shuffle will be that the dealer will get a natural on the first hand.

There are dozens of methods a card expert could use to control just one ace and one ten to be dealt to his own hand after the shuffle, and you will not see any of them. Just remember that a dealer should get a blackjack about once out of every twenty hands. If he gets a blackjack first hand after a shuffle, it's usually just luck. The odds against him getting a natural first hand after a shuffle twice in a row are more than 400 to 1. Be suspicious. If it happens a third time in a row, the odds against it having occurred due to chance are more than 8,000 to 1. Find another dealer.

Any time you feel uncomfortable about a dealer, leave the table. Don't take chances. If you think a dealer is handling the cards in an unnatural or suspicious manner, don't try to catch him in the act of cheating. You would probably be unable to spot it, and if you did, you could not prove it. Reporting suspected cheats to the casino will get you nowhere. Unless you can provide solid evidence—such as a hidden card beneath a shoe—and you have witnesses to back you up, you will be viewed as a troublemaker, a paranoid, a sore loser, or possibly a scam artist.

Most casino blackjack dealers are honest. If you are on a losing streak, don't blame cheating dealers. If you're playing for high stakes, you would be wise to seek a demonstration, and possibly a course of instruction, from a card expert who thoroughly understands cheating moves, especially those which can be used in casino blackjack. There are also books and videotapes available on the subject. (See Appendix.) Still, don't expect to see a good cheat. I've had personal demonstrations by some of the best card sharps in the world. I've had the moves explained to me in detail and performed in slow motion. All a card sharp can teach you is how to spot a sloppy or inexperienced cheat. An expert is undetectable. In any case, unless you have proof, your best defense is to quit that table at your first suspicion.

You should avoid getting involved in "private" illegal blackjack games. If you play for high stakes, and especially if you take junkets with other high rollers, you are liable to be invited to play in private games. This is risky. I know one pro who couldn't resist such an offer. He didn't realize he was being cheated until he'd lost $15,000.

Stick to the legal casinos. You're less likely to be cheated in a legal establishment. If you ever have even the slightest suspicion you are being cheated, quit the table. Most games are legit, but don't take chances.

♣♦♠♥

TEAM PLAY

A number of methods for partners and groups of players to benefit from card counting have been mentioned throughout this text. There is one other financial benefit from teaming up with other players that has not yet been mentioned.

When two or more players combine their bankrolls, with the agreement that the team will share all wins and mutually absorb all losses, then each member of the team may size his bets as if the team bankroll were his personal bankroll. The reason for this is that when more than one player works from a common bankroll, the effect on fluctuation is the same as if one player were playing very fast.

A few criteria must be met in order to achieve this team benefit. Most important, you must keep in close enough contact with all team members to reassess your bankroll frequently. Each team member cannot go off separately for 10 hours of play. You should meet every two hours or so to compare notes. If some drastic change in the team bankroll has occurred, everyone must adjust their bet-sizing accordingly. Some prearranged signal should be devised so that any team member who suffers a sudden significant loss may inform the other team members of this. One team I know used a $26 bet to signal any urgent team meeting. The player who was calling the meeting would simply place a $26 bet at each table where one of his teammates was playing.

Team members should not socialize inside the casinos. Many teams have been broken because a casino identified a single member as a card counter. All of the known cohorts of an identified counter become suspect, and are subsequently watched.

Team members should not play at the same table, unless this is necessary (such as for a depth-charging strategy). If you play at the same table, then you must all size your bets the same as if one player were playing multiple simultaneous hands. You will not reap the full benefit of your combined bankroll.

You must trust your fellow team members, and you should all test and drill each other. Never team with a player whose abilities or honesty you question.

All financial considerations must be worked out, on paper, beforehand. Dividing wins and losses can be difficult when various team members contribute different amounts to the team bankroll, play various numbers of hours, and win and lose various amounts of money. Most teams handle these factors according to methods originally devised by Ken Uston's teams (see Appendix).

To keep the bookkeeping simple, you would be wise to separate each player's contributions to the team according to bankroll, hours, and win/loss.

On one ledger, list each player's bankroll contribution. You may have a six-member team, with three members making no contribution, two members contributing $5,000 each, and one member contributing $10,000. Most teams judge this bankroll contribution to be worth 50% of the total team win. If the team doubles their $20,000 bank, then automatically 50% of this win ($10,000) would be divided proportionately among the three contributors to the team bankroll. The contributor who put in twice as much money as either of the other two would likewise take twice as much of this win.

If the team were to suffer a $10,000 loss, these three bankroll contributors would have to absorb the entire loss, in proportion to their respective contributions. It is because these team members are putting their personal money at risk that they enjoy such a sizeable proportion of the win.

A second ledger is kept with the total hours played for each player. The time contribution is worth 25% of the win. If the team won $20,000, $5,000 of this win will be divided up according to how many hours each team member played. You may have a six-member team, where one member contributes to the bankroll, but does not play, while five members play various numbers of hours. In this case, only those who put in time at the tables would take a portion of this hourly payment, equal to the proportion of time each member spent at the tables.

A third ledger records the total win or loss of each player. The personal win contribution of all players is worth the remaining 25% of the total win. Players whose net result has been a loss, would take none of this win. Those players who have won money for the team divide up this 25% of the total win in proportion to their personal wins.

There are a few other considerations which may enter into the division of team wins and losses. It must be predetermined how expenses will be handled. Players may either agree to absorb these personally, or the team bankroll may cover all, or certain specified, expenses. Some teams occasionally agree to pay new or inexperienced players a flat hourly rate off the top of the team bankroll.

Most important, it must be decided beforehand exactly how and when the team is to break up, and the wins and losses divided. Weeks of planning can be ruined if one major bankroll contributor decides to pull out suddenly. Arguments can be avoided by settling these matters beforehand.

It must be mutually agreed who will handle the money, the bookkeeping, etc. Virtually every team operates differently. The most successful teams are the most businesslike.

Team play can be more fun, more profitable, and less risky, if the team members handle all aspects of the work and play with care. The most important factor is mutual trust. Never team with anyone whose honesty you question.

♣♦♠♥

APPENDIX

TABLE ONE:

COMPLETE BASIC STRATEGY

S = STAND

H = HIT

D = DOUBLE DOWN

$ = SPLIT

¢ = SURRENDER

STAND

	2	3	4	5	6	7	8	9	X	A
17	S	S	S	S	S	S	S	S	S	S
16	S	S	S	S	S	H	H	H	H[1]	H
15	S	S	S	S	S	H	H	H	H	H
14	S	S	S	S	S	H	H	H	H	H
13	S	S	S	S	S	H	H	H	H	H
12	H	H	S	S	S	H	H	H	H	H
A8*	S	S	S	S	S	S	S	S	S	S
A7*	S	S	S	S	S	S	S	H	H	S[2]
A6*	H	H	H	H	H	H	H	H	H	H

* (See Double Chart for Soft Doubling strategy)
(1)   Stand with 3 or more cards totaling 16.
(2)   SINGLE DECK: If dealer hits soft 17, hit A7 Vs. A.
      MULTI-DECK: Hit A7 vs. A.

DOUBLE DOWN

	2	3	4	5	6	7	8	9	X	A
11	D	D	D	D	D	D	D	D	D^1	D^2
10	D	D	D	D	D	D	D	D	H	H
9	D^3	D	D	D	D	H	H	H	H	H
8	H	H	H	D^3	D^3	H	H	H	H	H

SOFT DOUBLE DOWN

	2	3	4	5	6	7	8	9	X	A
A8	S	S	S	S	D^4	S	S	S	S	S
A7	S	D	D	D	D	S	S	H	H	S^3
A6	D^3	D	D	D	D	H	H	H	H	H
A5	H	H	D	D	D	H	H	H	H	H
A4	H	H	D	D	D	H	H	H	H	H
A3	H	H	D^3	D	D	H	H	H	H	H
A2	H	H	D^3	D	D	H	H	H	H	H

(1) EUROPEAN NO-HOLE: HIT
(2) EUROPEAN NO-HOLE: HIT.
    MULTI-DECK: HIT
(3) MULTI-DECK: HIT
(4) MULTI-DECK: STAND

PAIR SPLITTING

	2	3	4	5	6	7	8	9	X	A
AA	\$	\$	\$	\$	\$	\$	\$	\$	\$	\$[1]
99	\$	\$	\$	\$	\$	S	\$	\$	S	S
88	\$	\$	\$	\$	\$	\$	\$	\$	\$[1]	\$[1]
77	\$	\$	\$	\$	\$	\$	H	H	S[2]	H
66	\$[2]	\$	\$	\$	\$	H	H	H	H	H
33	H	H	\$	\$	\$	\$	H	H	H	H
22	H	\$[2]	\$	\$	\$	\$	H	H	H	H

WITH DOUBLE AFTER SPLITS

	2	3	4	5	6	7	8	9	X	A
AA	\$	\$	\$	\$	\$	\$	\$	\$	\$	\$[1]
99	\$	\$	\$	\$	\$	S	\$	\$	S	S
88	\$	\$	\$	\$	\$	\$	\$	\$	\$[1]	\$[1]
77	\$	\$	\$	\$	\$	\$	\$[2]	H	S[2]	H
66	\$	\$	\$	\$	\$	\$[2]	H	H	H	H
44	H	H	\$[2]	\$	\$	H	H	H	H	H
33	\$	\$	\$	\$	\$	\$	\$[2]	H	H	H
22	\$	\$	\$	\$	\$	\$	H	H	H	H

(1) EUROPEAN NO-HOLE: HIT
(2) MULTI-DECK: HIT.

SURRENDER

	$\frac{9}{¢}$[2]	$\frac{X}{¢}$	$\frac{A}{¢}$[3]
16[1]	¢	¢	¢
15[4]		¢	
7,7		¢[5]	

(1) EXCLUDING 8,8
(2) SINGLE DECK: HIT
(3) SINGLE DECK: SURRENDER X,6 ONLY
(4) EXCLUDING 8,7
(5) MULTI-DECK: HIT

SURRENDER (HITS SOFT 17)

(same as above except)

	$\frac{A}{¢}$[1]
17	¢
16	¢
15	¢
7,7	¢

(1) MULTI-DECK: STAND

EARLY SURRENDER

	$\frac{9}{¢}$[1]	$\frac{X}{¢}$[2]	$\frac{A}{¢}$[2]
16	¢	¢	¢
15		¢	¢
14		¢	¢
13			¢
12			¢
7			¢
6			¢
5			¢

(1) EXCLUDING 8,8.
(2) INCLUDING 8,8.

TABLE TWO:
COMPLETE ZEN COUNT
SINGLE-DECK

This table is for depth chargers and serious fanatics only!

	2	3	4	5	6	(6)	7	8	9	X	A	(A)
STAND												
17											-14	(-12)
16	-16	-19	-22	-26	-23	(-27)	+16	+12	+9	0	+13	(+5)
15	-10	-13	-15	-18	-18	(-22)	+18	+16	+14	+7	+15	(+8)
14	-6	-8	-10	-13	-12	(-16)	+27		+21	+13	+22	(+15)
13	-1	-3	-5	-8	-7	(-11)						
12	+7	+4	+2	-2	+1	(-4)						
A7*											-4	(+15)
DOUBLE DOWN												
11	-24	-26	-28	-32	-34	(-34)	-18	-13	-9	-9	-2	(-4)
10	-19	-20	-22	-26	-29	(-29)	-12	-8	-4	+7	+5	(+5)
9	+1	-2	-5	-9	-12	(-12)	+7	+14				
8	+23	+16	+11	+7	+6	(+6)	+26					
7			+24	+20	+20	(+20)						
A9	+17	+15	+11	+11	+10	(+9)						
A8	+12	+6	+5	+1	+2	(0)						
A7	+3	-2	-12	-11	-13	(-18)						
A6	+1	-4	-11	-16	-25	(-25)						
A5		+4	-4	-12	-25	(-25)						
A4		+8	-2	-9	-21	(-21)						
A3	+21	+9	-3	-5	-12	(-12)						
A2	+15	+9	+2	-1	-6	(-6)						
SPLIT												
X,X	+19	+15	+13	+11	+11	(+10)	+26					

(Indices in Parentheses - If Dealer Hits Soft 17)
Insurance: Take at +4 True Count or higher.
7,7 vs. 10: Stand at 0 or higher.

* (See Double Chart for Soft Doubling strategy)

TABLE THREE:
COMPLETE ZEN COUNT
MULTI-DECK

	2	3	4	5	6	(6)	7	8	9	X	A	(A)
STAND												
17											−13	(−10)
16	−16	−18	−20	−24	−25	(−28)			+8	0	+13	(+5)
15	−10	−12	−14	−17	−17	(−21)			+13	+6	+15	(+8)
14	−6	−8	−9	−12	−12	(−16)			+20	+12		
13	−2	−4	−5	−8	−7	(−11)						
12	+6	+3	+1	−2	−1	(−5)						
DOUBLE												
11							−19	−14	−10	−9*	+1*	(−2*)
10							−14	−9	−4	+7*	+5*	(+4*)
9	+2	−2	−5				+7					
8			+10	+7	+4	(+4)						
A9				+9	+8	(+7)						
A8		+7	+5	+2	+2	(0)						
A7	+1	−4	−8									
A6	+2	−5										
SPLIT												
X,X	+17	+13	+12	+10	+9	(+8)						

<u>Insurance</u>: Take at +5 True Count or higher.
* <u>European</u> <u>No</u> <u>Hole</u>: Hit.

OTHER PRODUCTS AND SOURCES

Ten Recommended Books

If you are serious about playing blackjack for profit, no one book can act as a definitive guide. Card counting is a profession for some players, and as such, is a never-ending learning process. An extensive body of literature exists on the subject. As in any field of study, some of the available literature is valuable, some is so-so, and some is worthless. The ten books listed below are all unique and valuable. I do not agree entirely with all of the findings and opinions of any one of these authors, nor do they agree with each other. Nor is this list definitive. There are at least another dozen books on card counting of interest to the serious student. But these ten books provide an overview of the art of playing blackjack for profit from every perspective: the historical, the mathematical, the psychological, and the practical. These books are in alphabetical order according to author.

Turning the Tables on Las Vegas, by Ian Andersen (Vintage Books, 1976, 78). This is the best book available on casino comportment, cultivating an act, and the psychological strategies of winning at blackjack. The counting system is weak, but the rest of the book is invaluable.

The World's Greatest Blackjack Book, by Lance Humble and Carl Cooper (Doubleday & Co., 1980). An extensive textbook-style treatment of casino blackjack and card counting. The Hi-Opt I system is simple, powerful, and well explained.

The Theory of Blackjack, by Peter Griffin (GBC, 1979, 81). The most in-depth mathematical studies of casino blackjack and counting systems to be found anywhere. Unless you've had some advanced courses in probability and statistics, you won't understand all the math. But much of the text is written simply enough for the average player.

The Blackjack Formula, by Arnold Snyder (RGE, 1980). An approach to evaluating systems' gains according to table conditions for serious players. The approach is mathematical, but the math is clearly explained so that anyone can do it.

Blackjack for Profit, by Arnold Snyder (RGE, 1981). A simplified approach to evaluating profit potential according to table conditions. This is much like *The Blackjack Formula*, but without all the math.

Beat the Dealer, by Edward Thorp (Vintage Books, 1962, 66). The classic text on card counting by the man who first published a winning card counting system. The systems in this book are not recommended, due to their difficulty, but every card counter should read this book for a historical perspective on the game.

The Big Player, by Ken Uston and Roger Rapaport (Holt, Rinehart and Winston, 1977). An exciting adventure story of the original high stakes blackjack teams. If you're interested in team play, this book describes the ups and downs, and many of the original methods.

Million Dollar Blackjack, by Ken Uston (SRS, 1981). Extensive data on team play and training methods. The only detailed front-loading information available anywhere. Must reading for high stakes players. I wouldn't advise you to use Uston's Advanced Point Count System, since it's more difficult, but no more profitable, than the Zen Count. But this book is required reading for serious players.

Professional Blackjack, by Stanford Wong (Pi Yee Press, Morrow & Co., 1975, 77, 80, 81). Long-time pro, Wong, tells all with honesty and candor. Also contains the only detailed count strategy for playing "double-exposure" to be found anywhere. The Hi-Lo system is simple, powerful, and well explained. The techniques of Wonging are described. Much valuable data by a man who made a small fortune playing blackjack.

Winning Without Counting, by Stanford Wong (Pi Yee Press, 1978). Detailed warp strategies. Sections on tells, spooking, front loading, taking advantage of errors, cheating and more. There is no other book like this one. If you want to know every sneaky trick (legal and illegal) in the book, this is your guide.

Also of Interest:

The Development and Analysis of Winning Strategies for the Casino Game of Blackjack, by Julian Braun (1974, 75). Braun is one of the foremost computer experts on the game. This technical paper describes the results of his computer simulations of eight different systems, in single and 4-deck games, for one million hands each.

Blackjack Your Way to Riches, by Richard Albert Canfield (Lyle Stuart, 1977). This is a good level one system, well explained, along with some good information on casino comportment, camouflage, etc. The win rates are exaggerated, but the book has much to offer.

The Theory of Gambling and Statistical Logic, by Richard Epstein (Academic Press, 1967, 74). Epstein explains the logic behind the application of math to gambling problems. In depth and technical.

Experimental Comparison of Multiparameter Systems for Blackjack Strategy Variation, by John Gwynn, Jr., and Jeffery Tsai (1981). This technical paper describes the computer simulation of various multiparameter systems for more than 20 million hands each. The multiparameter approach to winning at blackjack is shown not to be significantly more powerful than the single parameter approach. (Multiparameter means keeping "side-counts" of aces, fives, etc., which some "advanced" systems recommend.)

Blackjack Supergold, by Lance Humble (B & B, 1979). This book has a lot of good tips for beginning players.

Casino Holiday, by Jacques Noir (Oxford Street Press, 1968). Now out of print, this book is a classic. The counting system is out-dated, but would still be good for single-deck games. Noir did some of the original computer simulations to test systems' gains.

Blackjack: A Winner's Handbook, by Jerry Patterson (G. P. Putnam's Sons, 1982). An excellent book for beginning players. Clear and concise. Good historical perspective. Extensive systems comparisons.

Blackjack's Winning Formula, by Jerry Patterson (G. P. Putnam's Sons, 1982). Another winner from Patterson, aimed primarily at beginners. Offers a simple approach to counting with the Hi-Lo system. Has a unique section on card counting for women (written by two women counters).

Playing Blackjack as a Business, by Lawrence Revere (Lyle Stuart, 1969, 71, 73, 75, 77, 78). A good, powerful, level-two system. Revere was an innovator. At one time this book was *the* definitive text for card counters. Now out-dated, but still valuable.

Winning Blackjack, by Stanley Roberts (SRS, Inc., 1971, 81). The 1981 edition of this book presents the Jacques Noir unbalanced ten-count as a more complete and useful system for blackjack games today. A good and easy system for single-deck games.

Cheating at Blackjack, by Rouge et Noir, Inc. (Rouge et Noir, 1981). A videotape available in ½" and ¾" formats showing the moves of the professional card cheat.

Recommended Periodicals:

Blackjack Forum: This is Arnold Snyder's quarterly technical journal for card counters. This is where the foremost blackjack authors, mathematicians, computer researchers and players discuss the latest methods and newest research on the game. Every issue is controversial, enlightening and entertaining. You can "listen in" while noted experts argue over the fine points of play. You'll find invaluable tips on which casinos are offering the best games, and which should be avoided. There are product reviews, a lengthy digest of recent blackjack news, and an extensive letters section. The subscription rate is **$24 per year ($30 overseas)**. Send your check or M.O. to: RGE, **414 Santa Clara Avenue, Oakland, CA 94610**

Boardwalker International: This is a magazine which covers the Atlantic City casino scene. Past issues have featured articles and/or interviews with Julian Braun, Lance Humble, Jerry Patterson, Arnold Snyder, Ken Uston, and Stanford Wong. Subscription rate: $22 (12 issues), 2515 Pacific Avenue, Atlantic City, NJ 08401.

Casino and Sports: This is a bi-monthly mag that primarily reviews new systems and books on casino and sports betting. Peter Griffin and Stanford Wong are both regular contributors. $15 (6 issues), GBC Press, Box 4115, Las Vegas, NV 89127.

Experts Blackjack Newsletter: This is a monthly newsletter published by *Gambling Times*, edited by author Richard Canfield. Contributors include Uston, Braun, Patterson, Snyder, Thorp, D. H. Mitchell, Stanley Roberts, etc. $60 (12 issues), 1018 North Cole Avenue, Hollywood, CA 90038.

Gambling Times: This monthly mag has always had good coverage of the blackjack scene with articles by the top names in the field. Stanley Roberts, one of the most controversial (and successful) blackjack authors writes a regular column. $29 (12 issues), 1018 North Cole Avenue, Hollywood, CA 90038.

International Gambler's Club Newsletter: Edited by author Lance Humble, this quarterly covers blackjack, horseracing, and sports betting. $24 (4 issues), International Gaming, Inc., Box 73, Thornhill, Ontario, Canada L3T 3N1

Jerry Patterson's Blackjack Bulletin: This is a new quarterly, formerly available only to graduates of Patterson's Blackjack Clinic. The emphasis is on practical tips for counters. $50 (4 issues), Casino Gaming Specialists, One Britton Place, Voorhees, NJ 08043.

Rouge et Noir News: This is a monthly newsletter of inside information on casino operations, junket reports, controversies, product reviews, etc. $40 (12 issues), P.O. Box 1146, Midlothian, VA 23113.

Stanford Wong's Blackjack Newsletters: Stanford Wong is one of the most innovative black-jack experts on the scene. He does his own computer research, extensive testing, in-depth casino reports, etc. There is always something new and valuable for pros in every issue of his newsletters. He offers 3 different newsletters:

Current Blackjack News: Detailed updates of casino conditions, number of tables, decks, rules, etc. Indispensible for full-time pros. $95 (12 issues), Pi Yee Press, Box 1144, La Jolla, CA 92038.

Nevada Blackjack: Letters from players, casino reports, etc., on blackjack in Nevada only. $21 (6 issues), same address as above.

Blackjack World: Product reviews, letters from players, and casino reports from around the world. $21 (6 issues), same address as above.

♣♦♠♥

For the most extensive catalogue of exclusively blackjack-oriented books and products, write to:

♠RGE♠ ™

414 Santa Clara Avenue
Oakland, CA 94610

(RGE carries a complete line of books, hard-to-find technical papers, home computer programs, videotapes, slide kits, training devices, etc.)